WHAT BLACK AND WHITE
AMERICA MUST DO NOW

WHAT BLACK AND WHITE AMERICA MUST DO NOW

A PRESCRIPTION TO MOVE BEYOND RACE

ARMSTRONG WILLIAMS
Foreword by Dr. Ben Carson

Hot Books

Hot Books may be purchased in bulk at special discounts for sales promotion, corporate gifts, fund-raising, or educational purposes. Special editions can also be created to specifications. For details, contact the Special Sales Department, Skyhorse Publishing, 307 West 36th Street, 11th Floor, New York, NY 10018 or info@skyhorsepublishing.com.

Hot Books® is a registered trademark of Skyhorse Publishing, Inc.®, a Delaware corporation.

Visit our website at www.skyhorsepublishing.com.

10 9 8 7 6 5 4 3 2 1

Library of Congress Cataloging-in-Publication Data is available on file.

Print ISBN: 978-1-5107-6422-4
Ebook ISBN: 978-1-5107-6423-1

Cover design by Kai Texel

Printed in the United States of America

CONTENTS

Foreword

The blatant and apparently senseless murder of George Floyd in Minnesota by an arresting police officer awakened our nation's sensitivities regarding race issues. In the aftermath of the George Floyd case and other well-publicized incidents of violent acts committed—seemingly unjustifiably—by law enforcement against African Americas, many Americans have engaged in heated debates about whether race relationships are getting better or worse; the answer of course depends on one's perspective and the environment in which one lives. In the Floyd case, which was captured on video, reactions ranged from anger to guilt to helplessness to many other things leading to an attitude that something must be done to end such blatant abuses of human rights by law enforcement. But what does that look like? On the other hand, divisive elements have eagerly sought to capture the energy associated with righteous protests surrounding the quest for human rights, and to further their own nefarious purposes. These forces tend to emerge anytime there is a national social crisis, because they want to further their own causes and really care very little about whatever the initial impetus for constructive change happened to be.

In his book, *What Black and White America Must Do Now*, Armstrong Williams, who is black, but has a wide range of multicultural life experiences and decades-long experience leading crisis management in government and industry, endeavors to impart wisdom and direction to a white audience who may not be equipped with the social and emotional tools to manage race relationships in times of social upheaval. This is not to say that everyone's life experiences are not equally valuable, but simply to provide another perspective for those who so desire.

It is not the color of one's skin that determines how they think and perceive the world; rather it is the environment in which they have lived and are currently experiencing. This became vividly apparent to me as a freshman at Yale. It was the first year that Yale accepted women, and it was also the first year that they had more than a handful of black students. Some of the black students, unlike many of the rest of us, had grown up in privileged environments and clearly had never interacted with other black people. Some of them would barely even acknowledge our existence, while others made every effort to immerse themselves in the black experience. The point being that it was their environment that shaped their personalities and not their race. This is the first thing that both white and black Americans need to understand.

Next, people must come to understand that lack of knowledge or awareness about other people's cultural issues does not automatically make someone a racist. We are all ignorant of one another to various degrees. And it is only by engaging in constructive dialogue, rather than assuming something about a person, that we all get to benefit from each other's diverse personal experiences and grow together as a nation. Unfortunately, society is becoming less understanding of this point and is quick to level charges of racism at even the slightest provocation. This in turn makes people act out of guilt or fear in ways that they would not normally act. These artificial actions further complicate interactions with members of other races. This book explores these kinds of issues in detail and lays out a framework that whites can use to approach situations involving racial tension more constructively and effectively.

The greatest thing that the reader will realize after reading this book is that we all have spheres of influence and we can begin the amelioration process when it comes to race relations by working within our own spheres of influence. We can be the change we want to see happen in the world. We can help people understand that we serve a loving God who gave us variety. Can you imagine how boring the world would be if everybody looked exactly like you, even if you're very beautiful or you're very handsome? Hopefully, we will all come to learn that we are all in the same boat and if part of the boat sinks, eventually the rest of it will go down as well. To keep the boat afloat and sailing to a positive destination let us all work on the thing that makes us civil human beings, and that is building good and constructive relationships.

—Benjamin S. Carson Sr., MD
Emeritus Professor of Neurosurgery, Oncology,
Plastic Surgery, and Pediatrics,
The Johns Hopkins Medical Institutions

Prologue

In the Marion, South Carolina, of my youth, all were aware of the deep legacy of racial divide that is embedded in the history, culture, and tradition of the region. The dim memory of slavery and reconstruction, the more vivid recollection of the civil rights movement, and the arduous walk away from a segregated society that followed are all deeply embedded in my memory and the collective consciousness of the South. Yet even in that midst, my own upbringing as an African American child was happy, secure, and the foundation of all that has since followed in my life. Those halcyon days of youth with my father, mother, and nine brothers and sisters in the rural South are the continuous blessing that have fueled the arc of my life now into the public square of political thought, commerce, and media. From that perspective, the convulsions that now grip the nation are particularly poignant and demanding of urgent remedy. The great British poet Alfred, Lord Tennyson pointed out that poetry is emotion recollected in tranquility. Likewise, I have stepped momentarily out of the fray and back to the family farm in Marion to view the current racial landscape in America, and in the book that follows will offer particular strategies for racial reconciliation and the full-throated expansion of freedom to all our people.

We all know the problems. We have all been recently and vividly reminded of the arrival of African men, women, and children to North America in chattels and against their will. The decades of forced servitude in slavery have been newly recalled. The disenfranchisement over decades, particularly in my native Southern region, of Jim Crow, poll tests suppressing voting, raw segregation, physical violence, and reigns of terror are freshly topical. Images of torrents of water issuing from fire hoses to knock down protestors, snarling dogs to hold them at bay and behind bars, and othe images of the civil rights era are now everywhere to be seen. Currently accounts of unvarnished police brutality selectively brought to bear on African American men caught by the unblinking eye of social media have enraged a nation. Here, as this summer begins, we find ourselves rocked to the core and once again staring in the face of our divided past and without a strategy for a path forward.

This, then, is our task. We need a direction of passage, a formula to follow, leading toward racial comity, equality under the law, and the deep harmony that only unfettered liberty can provide. This is the "unfinished work" President Lincoln spoke of on the field of battle at Gettysburg. This task he assigned to "the living" and now that is us.

From these fair fields of Marion, once worked by African slaves and now groomed these generations later by the sons and daughters of my parents, I have curated the observations and practical solutions for a modern America facing its age-old nemesis of racial division. This is our moment. President Jefferson and the Founders conceived a nation free from the servitude of monarchies and held out the dignity, sovereignty, and transcendent value of the individual. President Lincoln brought to the fold those African Americans who had yet to feel that warm embrace of Liberty. Now we are armed with the certitude that the elixir is human Liberty and the task that besets us is its full and untethered expansion into all folds and crevices of our society.

Senator Thurmond,
a Surrogate Father

As a black child growing up in rural Marion, South Carolina, during the 1960s and '70s, I never dreamed that one day South Carolina Senator Strom Thurmond—yes, that Strom Thurmond, the guy who famously filibustered against the passage of the Civil Rights Act of 1957—would eventually become my mentor. I'll never forget my father introducing me to Senator Thurmond one summer when we were working in the tobacco fields. Strom was speaking at the Dry Dock Seafood Hut in Mullins, South Carolina, as he customarily did during the harvest season when folks were in town to auction their tobacco crops.

My father thought that it was important that I meet Senator Strom Thurmond, this Dixiecrat, this former segregationist. I remember when we arrived, the luncheon was just ending. We were late because so much was going on with the farm that day.

I finally met him, and I walked up and extended my hand and said, "My name is Armstrong Williams." He said, "I'm Senator Strom Thurmond." I said, "Oh, everybody tells me you're racist."

He chuckled, and asked, "Well son, what do you think?"

I replied, "My father felt I should meet you and find out for

9

myself, and that I shouldn't always try to let others decide for me what a person is because a person can change."

Senator Thurmond said to me, "You seem like a pretty bright young man. Why don't you come to Washington, DC, when you go off to college and come intern for me during the summer and you figure out whether I'm a racist or not?'

That began my relationship with the former segregationist, not only from the needs of my parents, but from my relationship with Senator Strom Thurmond, who had more of an impact on my idea of race, racism, and all the isms associated with it.

My father always taught us that you cannot group people together. He wanted us to have a different experience than the ones he and his forefathers had endured over the course of human slavery, de jure segregation, and the civil rights movement. White people during those times saw us all as being the same, and they discriminated against us on the basis of our skin color. In fact, skin color discrimination was the law of the land in many Southern states until it was finally outlawed by the Civil Rights Act of 1964, which superseded all state and local laws permitting or requiring segregation. But because we were all classified as a "separate" race—separate from the human race—we had to have our own institutions, our own churches, our own social groups, our own colleges and universities. This sad state of isolation and separation was thrust upon us by the Founding Fathers, who did not have the courage to dismantle an amoral institution in America that my father felt would harm us for the rest of our lives.

Another lesson my father taught us is that everybody has a past, every sinner has a future, and everybody can change. Even Senator Strom Thurmond. At the time I met him in the early 1970s, Strom Thurmond was already almost seventy years old. Well anyway, I went off to college at South Carolina State

University, where I served as class president and majored in political science because I wanted to understand the dynamics of the civil rights movement, American history, and how it was reshaping race relations in the South. I had all but forgotten about Strom Thurmond's offer until I was about to go home from college, and the thought of having to return to work in my father and mother's tobacco fields and slopping the hogs scared me so bad that I figured working as an intern for the world's most notorious segregationist could not be worse than literally slaving away in the hot South Carolina sun. So I reached out to him, and lo and behold, within three hours of my call to the senator's office, a lady by the name of Holly Johnson was on the phone and said, "Can you hold for Senator Strom Thurmond?"

He picked up and said, "You're the young man that called me a racist." He asked, "Are you ready to find out?" I chuckled.

I was still a teenager, and I said to myself, this guy's got to be kidding, he remembers that? What he doesn't remember is that I thought my father was going to knock my face off. My father threatened to slap me because he said I was disrespectful, but he understood. He liked my boldness and the fact that I was willing to stand up and ask those kinds of questions. He said it boded well for me. I told the senator that I was calling him because I wanted to work in Washington, DC, for the summer. It was my first trip to Washington, DC, and would mark the beginning of a lifelong journey where, almost forty years later, I am still proud to call my home.

Senator Thurmond took a liking to me. He would take me to the White House where I was able to meet President Reagan. I brought Richard Pryor to Washington, DC, because of Strom Thurmond, who had my back when people in government and administration did not want Richard Pryor to come after he made a commitment to speak at a celebration of Martin Luther King's holiday, but had recently been caught in a dire controversy after having freebased cocaine and setting himself on fire. Most conservatives, and especially black conservatives at the time, believed that inviting Pryor would make a mockery of civil rights and reflect poorly on President Reagan's commitment to the issue; they were afraid Pryor, and by reflection the president, would become a laughingstock.

But sure enough, Senator Thurmond called the president and told him to stand by my side, "because if this young man says Richard Pryor is not going to embarrass him and is going to give a straight speech, I believe him." Strom Thurmond believed in me, and I'll never forget something else he said to me. He said, "Young man, everybody who comes to Washington wants to be close to a senator, the president, or someone in power." He said just think, "you've got yourself a senator," and it was true.

The man was always kind, and he talked openly about his past. He said it's not that he felt that blacks were inferior or hated black folks. He said he did a lot of things that he regretted and felt ashamed of. But those are the times that he lived, and he said he changed because he wanted to do better. He had stood for segregation—as had his father and grandfather, and as was expected of him as an upstanding Southern gentleman. He had also had marital infidelities that led to several scandals and divorces. But at the late stage in life in which he and I developed our relationship, the senator was far more concerned with patching things up with his creator and making amends here on Earth. As a result of our growing relationship, Strom Thurmond began to support key legislation to provide enhanced funding for historically black colleges and universities.

A lot of people don't know this, but Senator Thurmond was a deciding influence in the Senate to make Martin Luther King's birthday a national holiday. When Dr. King's widow Coretta came to Washington to meet with him she was deeply skeptical of his motives, but she soon realized that he was serious and sincere in his openness to dialogue and action, and she thanked me for the relationship and having the vision and the courage to deal with the name-calling that people directed toward me because I was associated with a man who had a reputation as a notorious segregationist.

Over time our relationship deepened to the point where Strom became almost a second father to me, especially after my own dad passed away in the mid-1980s. Late in the evenings in his office, he would have me come by to talk to me about politics and point out people who were supposedly liberals who were standing up for black people, but were just as racist as one could be. I won't call any names, but many were on the Democratic side. He would say "Look at them and guess what they said to me in the elevator this morning. Guess what they said to me over breakfast this morning." He said people play a role, and just because somebody called themselves a Democrat, it doesn't mean they're all front and center for blacks, civil rights, and equal opportunity. He said, "but at least you know what I know." This was an eye-opening experience, to say the least. It reinforced to me the lessons my own father had instilled in me: never stereotype, and don't judge a book by its cover. Just because someone says all the right things in public doesn't mean he's your friend, and just because someone has been painted as a racist doesn't mean he's your enemy. If you can just dig a little deeper, withhold judgment, open up dialogue and communication, you just never know what treasure a relationship might reveal.

That more than anything formed my understanding of people; because of my parents, and because of Strom Thurmond

and the kindness he directed toward me. He was so empowering to my career early on because he was always a listening ear.
I'll never forget people used to laugh at me in the administration because they never believed Strom Thurmond was really
my friend or that we had that kind of relationship. I'll never forget I called him one day and said, I want to have a reception
and invite you to my place. I lived in a one-bedroom efficiency
apartment on Capitol Hill, a roach-infested place that only had
two rooms, including the kitchen and a tiny space for a bedroom
and a bathroom. I told him it would mean so much to me if I
invited all of the naysayers by, and if he would just show up and
show he was my friend, because he was all in the news since he
was the chairman of the Senate Judiciary Committee. He said,
"I'll do that for you, son, I understand how important that is."
I'll never forget on the day that it was happening, Dennis Shed,
who's now a federal judge and was his chief of staff at the time,
called and said, "You know, the senator's coming over, but he
wants to know what to say."

So I replied, "Let me think about it."

At that time, Barry White had a song out called "Change."
I called the senator back and I told him what the lyrics of the
song were. Sure enough, he said, "I will let everybody arrive first
because they're going to think I'm not going to arrive."

He said he would call me when he was downstairs, and
I should go down to get him at just the right time. Everybody
was there; the place was packed like sardines. The senator called
and said he was on his way. I was fidgety and excited. I went
down and got the senator and people were shocked. He came
to my apartment and he quoted Barry White, saying, "It's time
for change, everybody can change, even I have changed, and it's
because of this young man, Mr. Armstrong Williams, my pro-
tégé, that I continue to change."

People believed that I was really impacting Strom Thurmond and his views on civil rights. I remember he became a champion for civil rights, believe it or not.

He said to me once, "Listen, if you were not aligned with Republicans (I'm a third-generation Republican), you would not be in a position to help us change and do better. People need to have power no matter who's in the White House, no matter who's in Congress. Nobody should be left on the sidelines."

I write this to say, I have never in my life experienced racism. I said this to my family, my colleagues, my staff, and people around the world. Racism has had no impact on my life or my success because if it did, there's no way that someone like me could rise to become the second largest minority broadcast television owner in America. The things that I've been able to accomplish in life really stem from the fact that I refuse to judge people based on their skin and based on their past. I believe that people can change, and that people can do better. I judge people based on where I want them to be, not where they have been. That is my philosophy. Even with my other hero, David Smith, the man who gave me the opportunity to enter the broadcast industry, we never have discussions about race and there's nothing bigoted about our discussions. What amazes me is how much he cares about minorities, and how he wants to empower those communities, and how he feels we should do more in terms of charity. In fact, he's the one who has led the way.

I feel blessed that I have never been tainted by the prism of race, I've never had a bad experience with law enforcement, and I've never felt slighted or denied something because of my race. So as I write this book, *What Black and White America Must Do Now*, remember that my values have been shaped not by racism, not as someone who's experience bigotry, and not as someone who's angry and feels that I've been denied something because of my skin color. I firmly believe that regardless of what skin color the creator had endowed me with, I would still be who I am today and where I am today, because it's about how I see people—as human beings, each individually endowed with a special gift from God, not as a race, gender, or group.

So, I write this book taking into consideration all my experiences from people of all walks of life, and I love the fact that my parents were Americans who happen to be black. They experienced racism and bigotry. They talked about it, but they always said, "You will not drink from that trough of bigotry, racism, and discrimination." They would say, "You deserve your own path, your own clean slate, and a chance to allow your experiences—not those imprinted on you by society—to shape who and what you become." They said, "Don't allow what we've gone through, and what people appear to be, to shape you. You must wipe the plate clean and see where the world takes you."

I'm forever grateful to my parents for insisting that I inherit a world without prejudice. I'm not here to blame or to guilt-trip anyone or to call someone racist or malign and marginalize them. I'm really searching for why it is that most Americans have not had the experiences I've had. It is racist to assume just because someone who happens to look like they would have had to have at least experienced some form of racism. I know some people will say I'm in denial, that I didn't give power to it; they'll say it doesn't make any sense. However, people can say whatever they want to say. I know what my life is. There are people who can testify what my life has been. This is my life and I tell the story and I write this book based on the foundation of those experiences.

Introduction

With American society experiencing unprecedented social upheaval and divisions along the lines of race, religion, and class, there seems to be a cacophony of voices either commanding or forbidding certain types of speech and activities on the part of whites to either prove they are not racist or demonstrate solidarity with the slogan "Black Lives Matter" (BLM). However, for many whites who want to be supportive of the cause of preventing police brutality and corruption (a common aim among people of all races)—and of civil rights and social justice more broadly—doing so under the auspices of BLM poses some significant values conflicts.

Furthermore, the calls for social justice have, in many cases, involved other forms of protest, including the desecration and removal of federal monuments and symbols, as well as calls for "kneeling" or otherwise protesting during the national anthem and other patriotic displays by attendees of sporting events and other entertainment venues. To many in white America, especially those who may have close friends and relatives who have served in the military and died protecting our country, this form of protest seems like an utter repudiation of the values for which our uniformed defenders fought and died. They gave the most sacred thing one could give, life, to ensure that we have freedom, justice, and equality.

So, to have those symbols sacrificed on the altar of political correctness seems to be a bridge too far. So the question this book seeks to address is: How can whites empathize with the cause of social justice and yet stand up for the symbols of sacrifice for freedom and equality that, in the eyes of many, make such a cause even achievable?

Along with calls to align themselves with the term "Black Lives Matter," we also hear calls to implement drastic policing reforms, including disbanding the police forces in major cities. In some cities, the local governments are considering "defunding" the police and directing taxpayer resources to other social and economic priorities. How is it possible for whites and blacks who may be taxpayers, homeowners, and business owners, who rely upon the police to maintain order and protect life and property—especially in the context of recent riots and looting—to have a conversation about police and justice reform without throwing out the baby with the bathwater?

If anything, we need a more robust, more professionalized police force equipped with the educational, social, and communications skills to serve an increasingly diverse population. We need more and better policing, not less and better, and with more unique qualifications and resources to get into this place of power.

How do we frame that conversation in the context of social justice to empower and reform our police force when we are willing to allow a few bad apples to corrupt the entire perception of those put here to protect and serve the citizens of this great country? How do we frame this question and approach it with pure intent when we make irrational decisions to cut funding to the very institution that held some level of accountability to values and laws for us all to build on?

To begin with, we are no longer talking about a few bad apples. We are talking about a rotten barrel. For too long, police and their unions and political backers have used the policing powers as a shield to violate American's civil rights and human rights. I am not referring to a particular race here. Blue lives do not matter because blue is not a group of people; it is merely a political construct.

There should never be a political constituency that represents itself as "law enforcement." Why is that? Because we herald our men and women in uniform as representing all Americans. After all, if we do not consider rituals of respect for law enforcement and the military to be "political acts," but merely patriotic ones, why should law enforcement have an identity separate and apart from the country at large? Let us agree that no one's black and no one's blue because we are all equal under the law, and no one should be made "black and blue" by the unjust and violent treatment from those whose job it is to protect and serve us. The fact is, we desperately need greater law enforcement accountability, or we seriously risk losing legitimacy.

On the other hand, during this time of the privileging of "black lives," a lot gets lost in the cacophony and madness of the mob. It is as if we are trying to drown each other out by trying to be the loudest voice, rather than the most reasonable and practical one. One particularly fraught narrative that seems to be emerging from this moment is that somehow whites are "mere spectators" in the quest for social justice in the age of Black Lives Matter. Some prominent pundits have suggested that whites curtail their efforts to reach out to blacks, show their support publicly, and just shut up. Nothing could be more dangerous or unproductive. In fact, whites make up the majority of the

American population, and their input on issues of mutual concern such as civil rights is not only welcome but essential if we are to make any progress.

We sorely need to begin an honest dialogue between people of different backgrounds to hash out different perspectives and arrive at mutually beneficial solutions. Of course, in keeping with the character ethic espoused by Steven Covey in *7 Habits of Highly Effective People* (and others), it is generally better to understand others before seeking to be understood. However, both listening and speaking are part of the process of getting to win-win, which is what we all want.

You need to make your voices heard, but we cannot merely shout and raise a fist, and we cannot in the same sentence turn around and stew quietly in hate either. We must speak out in a way that can be heard. Justice is a cold word when it is limited to a divided spelling, but when it is unified as one word, it is pronounced Just-Us, and that qualifies all voices to be heard, then qualified action must be taken.

Justice is a common cause, and if you follow BLM, then you see that it has also been corrupted to prove a point that cannot be heard as it has been spoken and intended. For example, there have been egregious instances of police abuse of white citizens (the Daniel Shaver case in Arizona; the botched no-knock police raid that killed Rhogena Nicholas and Dennis Tuttle in Houston in January 2019) that have not garnered the same national outrage and public backlash that the George Floyd or Ahmaud Arbery cases have. Moreover, that is sad because it did not involve a white person killing a black person. This disparity highlights a significant problem in terms of our values' alignment if we are genuinely attempting to move toward a more just society. We have to start somehow breaking away from making everything about black and white. We need to be equally out-raged whenever there is an injustice.

Our perspective must be less focused on the victim's race and more on our shared human dignity. We all possess this human dignity. We were all born into it, and somewhere along the way, we were talked out of it. However, as affirmed by our Constitution, these rights are inalienable—we cannot cede them to the state even if we wanted to. Human dignity is an inher-ent quality that resides and hides or is illuminated in all of us. Hence, the more we see it in ourselves, the more we will see it in others, and this will bring it out much faster than the aggression we are showing in our current state of belligerence as a country on fire.

As things stand now, there are far more instances of black criminals attacking and killing whites in this country. There are even more instances of black criminals attacking and killing blacks in this country. If one were to look at the numbers alone, one could surmise that blacks are infinitely more racist actors against other blacks than whites are—and certainly more racist than police are.

While these contextual issues—alignment with BLM, authentic communications, values, and identity conflicts—help to frame the conversation, the central aim of this book is to rec-ommend a course of action that white America can take to sup-port the cause of social justice in a way that makes us a better people and a better nation. It starts with assuming that most of us want what is best for our fellow citizens and finding ways to be kinder and more compassionate in general.

However, it also means that whites, especially those in cor-porate America or positions of influence in education and gov-ernment, can and should use their influence to open doors to opportunities for blacks and others who may feel marginalized. Certain advantages accrue to those who have worked hard to achieve the American dream. We who have benefited from our economic system should not feel ashamed of our achievements; instead, we should herald them as an example for others to follow and benefit from. We are not so much concerned with the plight of the poor and disenfranchised in terms of addressing them in ways that assume an ordained and inescapable plight; instead, we are concerned with the transformation of the poor into productive and wealthy citizens.

This is the core and fundamental difference between a generally conservative approach to outreach, philanthropy, and social policy and the liberal one. Liberals tend to be invested in creating programs for the poor that merely comfort them in their poverty, a cynical approach indeed. Conservatives tend to look more at how we can create opportunities, conditions, and incentives to move the poor out of poverty and into prosperity. So, when we look at social policies surrounding the criminal justice system and policing, we should also be looking toward wealth creation and civic participation—not more welfare and government subsidies—as the primary levers of societal transformation.

This process starts with our acknowledging that often, traditionally underserved groups do not know what opportunities exist because they have not been plugged into, or sought out, informal mentoring and support networks that exist and should serve all of us. Let us all strive to pull these young people out of their shells and into a new time, into all of these new networks that empower growth and prosperity, educating them that a new way has been paved; they just have not seen it or experienced it. We must not set our hand to the plow and look back; we must embrace a new future, or we will forever be bound to a history that no longer serves us. You do not have to take a knee to make a positive impact. Facilitating opportunities for leadership to show people all of the avenues of empowerment and economic advancement that are here for them are just as—or even more—effective in terms of making meaningful, positive social change than telling them to hold on to and fight for a past that no longer serves any of us in any way.

The knee-jerk reaction by the media and large corporations and institutions has been to erect virtual wannabe badges and other symbolic gestures—to signal solidarity with BLM rather than have the guts to stand up for what is morally and ethically right for all of mankind. This is especially true in the tech community and on social media platforms. However, those businesses have traditionally had a terrible diversity problem in terms of the numbers of qualified minorities they actually hire and promote and minority businesses they contract with.

It is time to call out the media's hypocrisy when it comes to practicing what they actually preach. Virtue-signaling in the absence of actual virtue is plain old phony and will not work as a real strategy for achieving meaningful change. If you want to preach about change, then you better be willing to show your Social Empowerment cards as to what you are doing to bring Unity and Cooperation to our society rather than division and competition that has historically done nothing but create war and division. I *am* done with this. It is time to call these media giants to the carpet for fueling the fire for their own grotesque personal gains.

As a practical matter, embodying actual virtues—compassion, honesty, prudence, temperance, courage, modesty—in our public and private lives is a significant contrast and counterpoint to the shrill virtue-signaling that has become all the rage. If we are consistent in these practices, we can, in the end, win the hearts and minds of our fellow citizens—irrespective of race, religion, or creed. Although this is a longer-term proposition, although you may not see immediate results, it will, in the end, prove to be the better course of action.

I am imploring us to reconsider whom we allow to influence our society. We have for too long now listened to radicals parroting phrases that they do not even really understand and taking actions against society that are destructive in such a way that they are actually doing themselves harm, not to mention the despicable destruction it is having on the community around them, including their own black brothers and sisters.

We must start to filter what we hear; we are so quick to believe everything social media states or that's on the news that we follow. Long gone are the days of evaluation, critical thinking, and verification. We will not succeed as a society of radicals following the lead of so-called leaders that are themselves terrified of a society that chooses to be freethinkers. We must free our minds from this propaganda and get back to thinking for ourselves, knowing ourselves, and speaking out from a place of self-awareness and practical insight.

I. Why Does Race Persist?

I am quite a skeptic when it comes to both racial determinism and racism because I do not believe race exists in any objectively discernible way. On a biological basis, we have phenotypes and genotypes, and even then, we cannot account for similarities of personality, character, education, environment, aptitude, and experience that all combine to make each of us a unique creature. There is no real biological feature to race—it is instead a social construct created by men that has been used in all sorts of negative ways to categorize and segment people based on nothing more than an apparently ingrained human predisposition to label, rank, and discriminate among each other—primarily in the contest for wealth and power. If it were not race, it would be something else—height, hair color, foreign birth, religious caste—or some other man-made way of dividing people based on some invidious difference.

The fact that we added the "ism" to the very word race indicates that some of us are looking for something to hold on to, something to be victimized by. Yet, the great black leaders of our time were anything but victims, and they would not for one moment think of stooping to the new age thug behavior we are seeing in our young adults. If you look up "ism," you will see that it has several meanings all within the same context, but only one I will mention here: "an oppressive and especially discriminatory attitude or belief." I think we can all agree with this. However, this has not stopped a significant proportion of men, women, and children from using race or racism as a means to cause division in our country. Let us get to the point that is at hand: Do I like that blacks were enslaved in the lifetime of my mother and grandmother? Of course not. Nevertheless, you know what? They persevered with a vision and a dream, and they overcame all adversity that rose against them just as Rev. Dr. Martin L. King Jr. and Rosa Parks did to show where they stood.

In today's day and age, bullying is the talk of the town in most schools. I hear nothing of segregation, and if we have evolved from the segregation of water fountains and restrooms to kids bullying other kids because of their own insecurities, then people, we are making progress. If there is one thing I know about life, we must not rush the evolution process.

I dare you to try to rush the process of growing a tree or a rose. I assure you that in your selfish process of rushing its evolution, you will kill it. We have lost the virtue of patience in this country. This is what we have done with our young people in this country: instead of focusing on family and their most influential years from one to seven years old, we have focused on rushing them into all these free programs set up to advance them to these expensive colleges that do nothing but create debt and mask the issues of their childhood that must be addressed before we can eliminate this issue with race and "ism" and the violence they are willing to participate in to overcome the burning feeling of needing to be significant to matter in this world.

Racism is a primitive form of thinking, the result of which has led to racial segmentation in the United States that continues to linger today. As a result, it has become ingrained in the psyche of many who see themselves and others through a racial lens, and in this lies the problem for all races. We are willing to make severe moves and grave consequential allegations on matters of which we often have little firsthand experience or understanding. This is a recipe for disaster.

Moreover, those who only see race treat others differently solely based on an exterior difference, and you also have those who view themselves as being separate from the larger group because of their exterior makeup, or equally as bad—they may discriminate against others merely because of their point of view. In fact, viewpoint discrimination may have actually superseded racism as the most pernicious form of discrimination prevalent in our society.

None of our egos like to hear that someone does not think like we do or is willing to present a point of view that challenges our own. However, the great sages of our time will be the first to teach that only a fool argues with a fool. Furthermore, anyone who wants to speak or advocate for a cause they do not have firsthand experience with is a fool, for they know not what they do not first seek to understand, therefore they will not be respected for what they have stood for. However, it could be argued that one does not need firsthand experience to act justly. As Adam Smith reminds us in *The Theory of Moral Sentiments*, we should treat others how we would expect to be treated if we imagined ourselves in a like situation. Race, racism, and even ideological biases cannot become the culmination of the human experience, yet it appears that they are. The greatest tragedy of this is that it is an indictment of the character and consciousness of a great many people.

As a result, individuals in camp one and camp two find themselves at a stalemate, begging the question of whether we should regulate race through the legislative process. We desperately want to believe that federal, state, or local government can stop racism. The answer to that question is simply no, and no matter how hard we attempt to use the government to orchestrate a perfect society, we will always come up short. While the government can attempt to regulate many things, it cannot regulate the human consciousness, for better or for worse. However, the government may regulate through policy that no legislation exists permitting legal discrimination. It can also mandate that no entity seeking to participate in commerce be allowed to discriminate based on race. However, that is the extent of what the government can do as it cannot regulate the heart, but it can encourage people to attempt to be better angels and strive for excellence while employing the best of human characteristics.

To be frank, the government was not put into place to regulate whom businesses could hire and fire; however, through regulation, the government must maintain that businesses hire people fairly and fire them with just cause. I would stand up to say that we as a country should be aware enough, courageous enough, and selfless enough to not do business with people who engage in any type of racism or discrimination. Why do we insist on blaming our government for everything when our government is just a flawed reflection of us as a whole—the government is you—it is merely looking back at you when you look in the mirror. Is it that the ugly truth is too much to bear? Admittedly, we have not become a society so feckless that we are unwilling to reflect upon our own shortcomings, but then again, that should come as no surprise because humans being like comfort but often choose it at the cost of introspection and self-awareness.

In his seminal essay, "Intellect," the great essayist and philosopher Ralph Waldo Emerson once wrote, "God offers to every mind its choice between truth and repose. Take which you please; you can never have both." As Emerson contends, we tend to oscillate between both extremes, untethered and unmoored like ships in a storm. "He in whom the love of repose predominates will accept the first creed, the first philosophy, the first political party he meets; most likely his father's. He gets rest, commodity, and reputation, but he shuts the door of truth. He, in whom the love of truth predominates, will . . . abstain from dogmatism . . . [h]e submits to the inconvenience of suspense and imperfect opinion, but he is a candidate for truth, as the other is not." Emerson's resolution of the human dilemma is both damning and hopeful in that it offers us a choice but does not require that we choose one or the other.

Unfortunately, we now have a society where the dogma surrounding race and racism have become big business. Purveyors of racial grievance find ready consumers among those who need a comforting boogeyman to blame their circumstances. That is not to say that race does not exist and that we should not continue to combat it when it arises. However, we diminish our efforts to stamp it out if we exhaust our grievances on petty acts of either benign or innocuous aggravation. People and businesses profit from racial grievances, which further compounds the overall problem with race built upon a system of division.

Here is a novel idea: how about we focus on cooperation. We can be, as Booker T. Washington famously said in his 1896 address at the Cotton States and International Exposition in Atlanta, "one as the hand in all things essential to mutual progress." To hasten along the path of real progress, we must seek cooperation, but we must also refuse to involve ourselves in anything that does not serve the greater good of all. Please do not misunderstand me; this does not mean we need to be "yes" men—quite the contrary. Just as we need to be slow to hire and quick to fire with our police force, we also need to be slow to adopt new ideas and careful to dismiss old ones because it is in old ideas that we learn what needs to be fixed and what we can become.

We must begin to understand and embrace the speed at which we can feasibly grow because it is harder to build than it is to destroy. We have come too far to revert to the barbaric tools to take us back to the Dark Ages, so I challenge myself and each of you reading this book to pull together and work on yourself not to slip backward.

I had a young man, whom I admire and appreciate very much, send me a photo tonight that struck a chord in me—as I am too a human. It stated his support to take down a historical monument in Washington, DC, that depicted Lincoln freeing the slaves. Everything inside of me wanted to appeal to him that this was a foolhardy endeavor, and to use every ounce of mental or physical manipulation to stop him. However, I had to acknowledge that he was free to hold his point of view, for what is freedom if we are not free to lobby for what we feel is right?

Then I asked myself, what would my ancestors have said if I spoke about this atrocity now with them? They would say, "Armstrong, do not be led by the past, yet be led by a vision of the future, a future where we all are free to be what God has destined us to be in a free-will universe, a heaven for all mankind if they so choose." With this sentiment in mind I must say that we do focus on the desired future, the future that we all seek of freedom for all, but a freedom that was earned through character and example rather than through barbaric display and complete disregard for those heroes who have gone before us and laid the ground for us to even be able to speak up today. For this, I tip my hat in honor of those who have given their lives for our freedom, and I implore those who will come after me to do the same in honor of those who laid this ground for you to be a freethinker, a free human being, and not a free radical with no regard for life, liberty, and the realization of happiness.

For those who are, in fact, racist, we must ostracize them and make it known where they stand. If they own businesses, we should be encouraged to stop all commerce with said entities and individuals to rid society of this horrid mindset. It is a way of thinking that goes to the core of who some people are, and that can only be regulated so much. We, as individuals, can form a framework of expectations for what we will tolerate and accept in our communities and overall society. As a society of religions, we may have failed to understand that science may reinforce our spiritual beliefs. Yes, I understand that religion and science have been seen as archrivals for countless centuries, but we have to admit that science and religion are now seeing eye to eye.

I would struggle to believe that anyone reading this book stands in opposition that our thoughts and visions do not have an effect on our future. I, for one, stand in the firm belief that they absolutely do. When we understand that we live in a field of energy, then we must understand that we, as a society, give energy to everything we focus on. We give power to what we focus on. Why do you think that big media wants you to divert your focus to drama and negative news? It is because it will expand and therefore they will expand, and they will do so at all cost. Not only at all cost, but they will do so in such a way that they are certain you will not think as a freethinker thinks; they are certain that you will follow the crowd and ride on the parroting chants of whatever brings significance to your life or the lives around you.

As tribalism increases and people turn further to groupthink, prejudice in various forms continues to expand and increase. We must focus on the individual because individualism fosters a society where all men and women judge one another solely based on their own individual actions or inactions, not on invidious distinctions such as race and gender stereotypes.

Intellectual considerations and debate over complex issues have ceded to basic groupthink. We must begin to understand that there is nothing more powerful than the collective consciousness. When your children throw their thirteenth birthday party celebrating life as a teenager, do you throw a huge party for them and give everyone under the age of thirteen a loaded gun and tell them that when the lights go off to celebrate and start shooting? Of course not, and such an idea would be ludicrous if anyone ever did. So why do we as a country pull together and support a collective consciousness of children raised in broken homes, with broken lives, seeking a place of purpose on this planet, yet set a foundation for the future based on fear and scarcity? Do we need to listen to our younger generation? Yes, we do. Do we need to sit them down and educate them on the feelings that they are having, that they are not alone, and teach them how human biology works? Yes, we do.

So my question is why do we instead join them in their display of insanity and display of cognitive dissonance toward humanity and not show up to love them and lead them to a new way of understanding, a way that Abraham Lincoln would have led them to, a way that all our great white and black forefathers led them to? Why? Why do we not do this anymore? Are we afraid of our own children? If we genuinely care for them, we must take responsibility and stop hiding behind them. If you believe in what they are fighting for, then, by all means, get off your derriere and fight, but fight from a place of knowing what you are fighting for.

Wisdom comes from experience that those who are among the unlived cannot possibly gain, which places the responsibility on those of us who have lived to teach our children the right values that will assist them with growing into productive adults. It is said that it takes a village, which I believe to be true if we are to raise the type of kids who will become adults who can lead our society to the next level. The problems we are experiencing today are a result of our own faults as adults and as a society. Our children will only be as good as the amount of time we instill in raising them and guiding their moral and ethical compasses.

Race and racism are man-made constructs that we need to deconstruct and eliminate if we are to ever move forward as a society. They were created to divide and conquer, and we must be intelligent enough to recognize this and correct it. The promulgation of our stagnation as a society can nearly be traced back directly to various forms of race and racism. Trace it back if you like, but please, let go of it. Holding on to it is no different from holding on to that one relationship that did not work out. I can promise you that the one will never enter your life because you are holding on to the past.

As long as we hold on to the past and continue to identify with a failed story we tell ourselves, we will never move into our desired future. Inevitably, our primary focus as human beings and as a society must be to continue to move toward a better and brighter future, so that one says we can arrive at a destination so foreign from whence we arrived that generations from now can look back and say, wow, look at what those of the past did to get us here.

You cannot live in a free society while permitting racism to exist. We must not base our estimation of people solely on their belonging to a group, any more than we should assume all members of a group think alike because a collective consciousness is dangerous without a leader that stands with a definite purpose for all mankind, not for one mankind but for all.

Groupthink is what permits racial prejudice because it encourages groups to view themselves as being superior to others; it fosters superiority based solely on race instead of judging people based on their ability, moral character, and ethical compass. Sure, as Emerson, said we could choose repose. However, why not be a candidate for truth?

Perhaps we will never be able to get over this sinister belief. It cannot be underscored enough that race and racism are among man's worst creations, and they are creations that we may not ever be able to destroy completely, but we should never stop trying to eradicate this evil. This group mentality has concord with the greatest armies—without ever raising a sword in the case of Gandhi, and it has also cost the lives of all men on the battlefield in the case of Custer. Neither party stands as right or wrong; we need both examples in life to be able to ask ourselves whom we choose to be. Who do I, as a currently free individual of the United States of America, choose to be?

You can stand for either-or, in this great country, that is your freedom and that is your right, but if you defer this too long, you will lose that right before you even know it. What are you, the sole survivor of democracy and freedom, willing to do to carry on what this country stands for or stood for? What are you willing to do to carry on that legacy to our children and continue to create a society that believes in promoting and supporting truth-seeking freethinkers?

II. Contemplate the Seven Truisms

The beginning of understanding—of true repentance and turning toward unity and harmony with black communities—begins first with the most important social institution man has known: the individual.

Through the years, I have pondered and explored the root causes of these perceptions and behaviors with my white brothers and sisters. White individuals can first identify with blacks' oppression and still confront their own acquiescence healthily in this struggle through seven truisms:

A. Acknowledge Your Confirmation Prejudice

There is more than a bias that haunts white Americans. It starts with a negative perception—call it fear, confusion, whatever—and festers and grows as the black individuals they know or see in public confirm in small ways some of the negative stereotypes that white Americans have heard or spread. This is a confirmation prejudice that is both an incomplete depiction of reality and dangerous to the cause of reconciliation. I have written before that this prejudice is rooted in some of the most original sins/failures since the dawn of man—pride and hate. The two feed off each other, and they can stain a soul and choke out any emotional opening for understanding someone who does not look like them.

I must also implore blacks to search for their current cultural structure and ask yourselves how we are representing our culture to the world. I think we will find that we can also do better; our children deserve better, in many cases. We all must rise to this challenge, both whites and blacks: this will bring understanding that we are only fighting ourselves, hurting ourselves; we are all fish in the same bowl.

Moreover, and this is the critical point here—look at fallen societies in the past; look at ancient Rome, ancient Greece, Egypt, and the rest. When those societies collapsed under the strain of their internal divisions—greed, prejudice, slavery, and corruption—no one escaped the collapse, not the peasant in the field nor the kings and noblemen in their country estates. If we put things in proper perspective, we will realize that we all are mutually dependent upon each other's success. There is no you, me, he, she, or they. This is us.

To begin widening their perspective, white Americans *must* first acknowledge their biases and be willing to surrender belief until they have developed better awareness and thinking tools. And how does one do that? Look for ways to challenge your perspective and gain real-time ground-level experience. Mother Teresa did not become Mother Teresa staying in her church and preaching about peace and love; she became Mother Teresa by taking her love to the streets. She did not take judgment to the streets—she took awareness, understanding, and love, and through her firsthand experience, she was able to shape and change the world. For example, if you believe that blacks are criminals, then I implore you to note the number of African

Americans you see acting in law-abiding ways throughout the day. Literally, count them.

Try this for a week or so, and then reflect on how many blacks you actually saw committing crimes. How many were just going about their daily business in a lawful and orderly way? Also, in an interesting reversal, I implore blacks and other races to take notice of whites that actually act out toward you in a state of racism or in a way that holds you back from being anything that you would like to be.

From what I have seen, America has gone above and beyond to favor minority business owners, minority students, and minority employees of all races and genders. America has reformed most of its foundation through empowering leaders to facilitate lifting up and empowering all minority demographics. But when you ask those demographics about these programs, they simply don't know of them because they have not been educated about them or have not sought them out. In many cases, many have been held in bondage with programs that don't require seeking of knowledge to expand. In many cases these programs, such as welfare, have been taken advantage of, and it's killing the impoverished people of our country.

Secondly, seek out better sources of information. For example, could crime correlate more closely with poverty or education than race? Do blacks with college degrees commit crimes at the same rate as both blacks and whites without college degrees? Try to dig a little deeper for answers and gain true experience, rather than accept blanket labels that cause us to jump to judgment of that which we don't understand.

Thirdly, discuss your opinions with others who may have a different perspective. Of course, this may be more easily said than done, but people are now open to these types of discussions. Be open to disagreement and discovery, and don't necessarily take a difference in perspective as a difference in intention. Assume all of us want the same thing, which is peace, harmony, and prosperity, and walk a country mile in that person's shoes and you'll see that truth is relative until it is experienced.

Name it! Claim it! Then immerse yourself in black culture as deeply as you can, experiencing it to your core so that we can walk in full awareness of one another.

B. Be Intentional

The second truism is related to the first—Be intentional. White Americans, set your mind to do this and stay the course. Seek it out. Better race relations do not just happen; they develop, and only after one is purposeful. It sounds simple, but it is not easy. You will be disappointed, I promise you, especially if you set out with many expectations. Instead, you must keep an open mind. Somewhere in your interactions with my brothers and sisters, someone will fail you or push you back to your confirmation prejudice. Resist. See us as you started individually from your mother's womb. Each with our own motivations and purposes simply composed of the sum of our environment and experiences; yet, we all share a tie that (should) bind us together as humans and Americans—a sense of shared community. The thing to remember here is that being white is not a character flaw; being black is not a character trait.

There are good and bad people from all walks of life, but that cannot be discerned from the color of a person's skin, but we can use the wonderful diversity of our society to know ourselves better. It is often by who we are not that we can best know ourselves. Without the perception of bad, how can we know ourselves as good? Yet we judge as if one or another is good or bad simply based on our values, and our values are a product of our completely different environments, yet rest assured we all want to do the best with the knowledge that we possess. Let's commit to leading all races into a place of knowledge where they are free to decide whom they choose to be from a place of the abundance of knowledge instead of a place of scarcity that forces them to be in survival mode all the time.

As some of the black protestors recently told a Colorado sheriff when he asked them what they wanted him to do the night of protests in that mountain town: "Walk with us!" White America must now walk with us. You don't even need to talk or say anything intelligent. Just walk with us, and in many cases, they did, and it was beautiful. Now I implore you to keep walking with us, commit to the process, to the journey with us. Let's walk until we walk together as One, understanding that we will never be the same, and we can celebrate that, but we can walk as One.

Let's put an end to tribalism. Set your mind to this and, collectively, things will start to change. While tribalism is a comfortable way of organizing ourselves because it promotes and reinforces shared values based on shared experiences, there has to be a function within tribes that connects us to the broader tribe—our cities, our states, our nation. Tribalism is not bad per se, but when it fails to connect to the broader society in a healthy way, it can become insular and self-defeating. Tribes have fought for centuries for power; we must eliminate tribal culture and just become one productive, progressive, peaceful culture that the rest of the world can observe and follow.

C. It's Not about You

You are probably scratching your head right now. Didn't Armstrong just tell me that change begins with me as an individual, then spread?

Yes, but never take yourself too seriously. Sometimes, it's

our own selfish lack of motivation that keeps us blind to seeking the experience of another possible truth. True empathy for the oppression of my people begins with humility as a whole. It's when we are meek in our spirit that we are more apt to learn and be teachable as a society. Meek doesn't mean weak—it's a gentle strength that patiently processes all that surrounds, then makes informed decisions that are absent of confirmation bias.

Rodney King, Eric Garner, Michael Brown, Laquan McDonald, Tamir Rice, Walter Scott, Freddie Gray, Alton Sterling, Breonna Taylor, and George Floyd—in each of these cases, and dozens more, officers made their encounters with these people of color about themselves. They held no regard for human life at that time; it was all about them, and this is just as much a cultural breakdown as we have discussed in our own culture when there is no regard for life, that starts in the environment of the family. This must change.

When we are hiring people to sit in places of power, we *must* thoroughly examine their childhood and deep roots of anger or family issues that they are harboring. We must know that they can handle the stress of the job, and we must have the backbone as leaders to hold individuals accountable when they show the first provable sign of lack of self-control. Slow to hire and quick to fire will save a lot of lives and unneeded backlash. We could have avoided a *lot* of the above catastrophes had we had the right leaders overseeing these police officers.

The moment Americans think this issue is more about their comfort, their safety, their way of life, we lose as a society. Yet this is beyond white-on-black crimes or specific instances of brutality. The same should hold for black-on-black killings, for black-on-white killings, etc. No one is exempt! No one gets a pass because of past events or in pursuit of reparations. It all must end, now.

D. Race Is Not Binary

Too often in America, white people view issues as a zero-sum equation: If they are winning, then I am losing. This should not be. Race (and racism) are not binary equations. If racial justice is flourishing, then that does not mean prosperity for whites is somehow diminishing. For too long, white Americans have viewed the rise of blacks in that manner. It's Philistine thinking, and once white Americans come to grips with this truism, we can take a huge leap forward for this community we all seek. As Rumi once wrote, "A candle never loses any of its light while lighting another candle. The light only grows brighter!"

What we should be thinking is that if each of us is better off, we are all better off. This goes against the grain in some sense because we tend to think of the sum of available resources in terms of a fixed pie, where more for some means less for others. But another perspective is to say that by empowering others, we grow our collective strength and that in turn creates better opportunities for each of us.

Another way of thinking about this—especially apropos to the protests and civil unrest that we see in the streets—is that extremes of wealth and poverty destroy the relative value of wealth. It does one no good to have all the money in the world if everyone else who is shut out of wealth and opportunity grows restive and resentful. Wealth and power become useless at the extremes because they tend to curtail the mechanisms of distribution that we need to have in place in order to have a successful society. While we are individuals, we do not live in a vacuum.

E. Expect More: Anticipate Racism, Then Act

Another way for white individuals to act proactively on race is to expect more of yourselves in your interactions with people of color. Do better. Expect better. Seek out and find the best in your black neighbor, your black pastor, your black bank teller, find the beauty in the contract with one another and learn how to celebrate it. We are all around you, white America! Be aware of that fact, then embrace it, but embrace it through new eyes, eyes of experience. Also, anticipate. Anticipate that someone somewhere would seek to show hate toward a person only because of their skin color. Choose to be acutely aware of it. Anticipate it—live every day in understanding the expectancy of such personal disregard.

Then respond. Respond in a way that reflects the change you desire to see. Act as such to root it out. Shut it down at work, at church, in your own home through congruence of your values and actions. Your children are sponges and mirrors—they absorb whatever behavior you condone and applaud, and they reflect that behavior when they're outside your watchful eye. Anticipate that and lean in to correct those small tinges of racism and prejudice whenever and wherever you encounter them. Our first experiences with race usually start in the home, so we must reintroduce core family values to our children and then give them the freedom to be freethinkers and to decide, with proper knowledge, who they want to be. We will not properly inform our children by injecting them with our own unresolved hate, prejudice, and anger—deep-seated hurt that we are often unwilling to acknowledge and evolve through. We *must* stop this carelessness and save our children from ourselves. We must change as a generation so that we do not pass this generational curse of racism to the next. It's never too late until it is.

F. Acceptance Does Not Always Mean Agreement

I promise you black people and white people will not always agree. We will not see eye to eye—on any issue that our society faces. It's natural and who we are as human beings. My white friends here in DC are die-hard Washington Redskins fans. They groan every time I proudly wear my Dallas Cowboys regalia. They don't agree with me, but they do accept me. I don't always agree with President Trump, and he certainly doesn't always agree with me. But he accepts me, and that acceptance is a form of respect and mutual admiration. Realize that just because you may differ with someone, that doesn't make him or her your enemy. Nor should we merely tolerate each other. Mere tolerance can cause resentment as unresolved and unexpressed tensions can fester beneath an outward veneer of tolerance. Instead, we must move to true acceptance before we see equality, and acceptance can only come through understanding.

White Americans must realize that acceptance does not always mean agreement. We can disagree on almost any policy or socioeconomic issue. But that does not mean it should lead to hate or prejudice, from either side of the table.

To my white friends, go ahead and embrace this truism. It's liberating! We can disagree! We can argue, cuss, and bicker over ways we all want to see this nation and this world improve. But don't dismiss me or disrespect me because I'm black; any more than I dismiss your opinions because you happen to not look like me. And for that, I promise to lead my people to do the same, and then we shall walk together as One.

G. Beware (and Ignore) the Fourteen Percent

I'm no longer a cultural anthropologist, so I have no scientific or statistical evidence to support my fourteen percent claim, but in my decades of working and traveling around this country, I've noticed that there is always a small contingent of Americans who will always fight reconciliation and racial justice. It's in their blood. They will never know differently. I call them fourteen percent, and we, as a country, must beware of them yet ignore them. I implore you to use this tiny, futile percentage as a gentle reminder of how far we have come through time, and the accepting individuals and accepting culture we are committing now to being. Let this contrasting percentage be the micro opposite of the macro that is deciding to walk into a future together as One Unified Society, choosing daily through this contrast as to the Free Country that we represent to the world.

The media will always cover these radical views as long as we pay attention and empower them to do so. Let's remove our attention from this regime, just like any good general would do, cutting off the lifeline supply to starve the enemy out, and watch the racism go away. It only remains because we keep giving energy to it; we as a whole are single-handedly keeping it energized. The media publicize and sensationalize the Klan, the antifa, the supremacists, you name the group, and there will always be a small remnant of Americans who will fight this movement for positive social change.

Think of it another way: for every seven Americans who agree the time for change has come, there will be one or two who say, "no way." Again, not a scientific discovery, just human nature that teaches there is always one who cowers in fear of the future and in fear of change.

This fourteen percent are social outliers—agents of conformism whose souls died long ago on the altar of ignorance and bigotry and laziness. And if we acknowledge now that they will always be lurking in the shadows, pulling white Americans back into the fold of the "good old days," then we can be prepared to combat that outdated vision. To be clear, returning to a period of racism and segregation will not Make America Great Again.

III. Resolve to Change

It is not events that disturb people,
it is their judgments concerning them.
—Marcus Aurelius

A. Why Must We Change?

All change is born out of necessity. America herself was born out of the necessity to form an independent nation, free from England's despotic rule. American colonists had long griped about onerous laws, usurious taxes, and arbitrary punishments they suffered under British colonial rule. However, what was it that, on July 4, 1776, *necessitated* a formal Declaration of Independence? What had changed?

Surely, as the Founding Fathers put it, "prudence will dictate that governments long established should not be changed for light and transient causes." So whatever reasons compelled them to want to throw off the mantle of the British Crown were not "light" or "transient." The colonists had resisted change for quite some time, not because they were exactly happy about the state of affairs, but because they finally recognized it is human nature to be "disposed to suffer, while evils are sufferable than to right themselves by abolishing the forms [of government] to which they are accustomed." Change is often *scary and painful*.

Even a bad status quo, as behavioral scientists have demonstrated, is often preferred over an uncertain future, and this is where our suffering sets in. Everyone is afraid of what they do not understand, and it's simply laziness that we don't first seek to understand before we move forward with so-called boldness to be understood. When an individual or society moves forward on a subject matter without a clear understanding, you can be sure that that matter will not be quietly and peacefully resolved without bloodshed and many years of war.

The nation is seriously asking itself whether we are still free, whether the petty slights, the naked abuses, the impenetrable bureaucracy we are experiencing is worth rising up in arms and overthrowing the status quo. Americans are generally a peaceful and law-abiding people; we are tolerant and understanding. But then we are tense and uncertain about our status, and one wonders whether the tensile strength of our social fabric might not be frayed to its utmost endurance.

Although uncertainty abounds, there *always* comes a time "when, in the course of human events, [change] becomes necessary." For the colonists, it was the culmination of a "long train of abuses and usurpations," which "evince[d] a design to reduce them under absolute despotism." That is, over time, the petty abuses of the British Crown had added up to what they saw as a *systematic* abuse of their God-given and inalienable rights to "life, liberty, and the pursuit of happiness." And that situation compelled them to rise in opposition and change their system from within.

It is as if Americans found themselves in the position of the great tragic figure Hamlet, who asked whether it was "nobler in mind to bear the slings and arrows of outrageous fortune, or to rise up in arms against a sea of troubles, and, by opposing, end them?" And such was the birth of the great American experiment, one that has yielded untold prosperity and shone a beacon of freedom across the globe over the last two and a half centuries.

Yet, here we find ourselves acting out as victims of society instead of leaders of the world representing freedom of speech and our progress to equality for all mankind. We have become the laughingstock of the planet because we have lost our core values, we no longer know who we are, and our leaders have lost the backbone to stand up and be the light that this country was built on and needs in this darkest of times. We find ourselves ravaging our country and terrifying our people in the cause of being heard, all in the name of so-called equality and peace. Our forefathers would be ashamed of the cross that we have taken up in the name of freedom.

Arguably, America is now at a similar crossroads as to how to come to a resolution for all. With a mountain of cultural values so vastly different from the leaders that separated us from the British Crown, how can we prevail? So, there are myriad cultural values that arise out of a love of freedom that avails us of a diversity of thought which the colonists would have envied. After all, the vast majority of them had found themselves cast out of the old continent for daring to question the divine right of kings, for adopting a scientific skepticism about the status quo, for daring to question whether the earth was flat. They took real chances defying the status quo, daring to exchange certain repose, even if unrewarding, for an uncertain truth. And they saw America's bounty as their reward for taking those risks, for forsaking the warm hearth of social connection.

White America is starting to wake up to the fact that what they may have considered isolated and unrelated instances of police abuse have, over time, become so systematic and embedded in our *country* that they demand to address the entire social structure. When whites see a Trayvon Martin, followed closely by a Philando Castile, an Ahmaud Arbery, a Breonna Taylor—they know instinctively that there is something deeper at issue.

It goes beyond just one bad cop; there is a system in place that sanctions these kinds of extrajudicial killings under the color of law.

And with such a strong focus on black injustice, we must ask ourselves what other injustices we are carelessly dismissing that create incongruence in our so-called righteous actions. We know that injustice does not merely root itself in one place and among one segment. If there is a systemic problem, it is eventually going to be a problem for everyone, and the thinking, conscientious people among us know this implicitly. It is not as if Hitler first came and carried the Jews (and many others) to the concentration camps and gas chambers all at once. As German Christian minister Martin Niemöller said when it finally dawned upon him that Hitler was not just radical, but also totally evil:

> First, they came for the socialists, and I did not speak out—because I was not a socialist.
> Then they came for the trade unionists, and I did not speak out—because I was not a trade unionist.
> Then they came for the Jews, and I did not speak out—because I was not a Jew.
> Then they came for me—and there was no one left to speak for me.

Whites know that they cannot stay silent anymore because in the tyranny they see exhibited against blacks, they see a threat to their own freedom and the freedom of others. If systemic racism and law enforcement think they can get away with such blatant abuses of human and civil rights for one group of people, what makes you think they won't eventually get around to doing it to you? And the fact is, whites have, in many cases, been almost too willing to give up their constitutional rights because they are overly trusting of the government. Our Founding Fathers would not be pleased by our lack of skepticism and righteous indignation. They would have urged truth over repose.

If they do not speak up now, it may be they who next face the lash of oppression and the alienation of their God-given rights. Civil rights in this context places both black people and white people and all other American races in a mutual struggle to ensure that America lives up to her core values. After all, the same righteous indignation that led thousands of Americans to oppose the drastic, economy-killing stay-at-home orders during COVID-19 is the same spirit of revolutionary freedom that is driving people of all races to the streets to oppose and condemn police brutality. This is not merely a fad; it represents a sea change in public sentiment. Just a year ago, BLM was considered a dirty word, almost as dirty as, say, KKK. Now, it has become, for better or worse, the lingua franca of the public discourse.

And in this respect, our Founding Fathers would be proud: we are not willing to just lie down and take the government's word for it. We believe that injustice, even if it enjoys the color of law, must be opposed. We believe it is nobler in the mind to endure the slings and arrows of outrageous fortune, but when they become unbearable, it is our American duty to revolt against them. Protest is American as apple pie. But it will be all for naught if we do not check in with each other, if we don't unify against the common enemy of freedom that is tyranny.

But for us to even consider unifying, we must step out of victimhood. We are not victims but potential champions. If we do not address these offenses against liberty and life, we not only risk losing all of the progress we've made, we also risk reverting to a dark age of ignorance and oppression from which we as a nation believed we had escaped centuries ago. Today's challenges are different from the challenges our ancestors faced when founding and frontiering this country into the magical place it is today, but they are no less significant. Nevertheless, we find ourselves somewhat ill-equipped to deal with the duties attendant to maintaining our Democracy because we have failed to teach our young generation about the perils that our founding ancestors went through to create this place of abundance. They have enjoyed some of life's greatest luxuries and amenities such as having water on tap, indoor plumbing, a roof over their head, and more programs to help and assist them than one can count. We have been so blinded by our own need for significance that we failed to remember that the price of freedom is eternal vigilance.

B. Change Starts with the Individual

America's most significant social innovation was to vest the power of government in the hands of the governed. This was derived from a theory of individual rights that was a novel concept at the time of America's formation. Across most of the world, rulers held absolute power, and even in constitutional monarchies in places like Germany and England, absolute power was vested in the legislatures. The United States was the first nation to say, no, everyone has *inalienable* rights, including life, liberty, happiness, and a host of other enumerated rights outlined in the Constitution and the Bill of Rights. As it stands right now, our rights, all of our rights, are being stripped away like a boiling frog thinking he is having a day at the spa—next thing he knows he is frog soup. We have to wake up, we have to regain our power as a democracy that stands for freedom even if it is against our own people, white or black, but it has to be done from a framework of unity and constructive engagement; this is what will bring the power back to the people.

The other genius of vesting rights in the individual is that we are not grouped by the government in castes or classes, as was done in places like India and feudal Europe. Each American is considered equal under the law, and the opportunities available to each are available to all. People must ultimately be treated as individuals. The notion that *all* blacks or *all* whites are this or that is absurd. People are ultimately responsible for themselves and their families. The nation's core historical values are Christian, and we need to act on that: Galatians 6:2: "Bear one another's burdens, and so fulfill the law of Christ"; Matthew 22:39 (the Great Commandment): "Love your neighbor as yourself"; and the Golden Rule, Luke 6:31 and Matthew 7:12: "Do unto others as you would have them do unto you."

Addressing this book to "white" America is somewhat of a betrayal of that ideal, just as Jim Crow and de jure segregation were betrayals of the ideals of individual freedom that are enshrined in our country. So, before we begin to address matters in terms of one "race" or another, it is incumbent upon us as self-sovereign individuals to begin to look at what we can do to effect change: first within ourselves, our families, our communities, and then ultimately as a society. We must begin to work on refining and improving our character so that we can ultimately expand our small circles of influence to meet our wider areas of concern. We absolutely must regain our culture of family values and move to a place of cooperation, or we will remain in this growth spurt until our bones break.

Edward Everett Hale, a social reformer and Unitarian minister, spoke out eloquently against the evils of slavery and wrote extensively in support of the Union army during the Civil War. He came from a long line of men of conscience. His greatuncle was Nathan Hale, the famous American spy who infiltrated the British Army during the Revolutionary War and was later caught and hanged by the British for treason. Like his great-uncle,

Edward loved liberty and despised despotism, so much so that he risked his life in service of freedom. Hale understood the founders' motivations for vesting political power in the individual and believed slavery was a human rights atrocity and a threat to individual liberty among free people.

Although Hale was an American patriot, he was especially conscious of individual liberty—and the spirit of agency it promoted. His famous quote embodies that spirit:

> *I am only one, but still, I am one. I cannot do everything, but still, I can do something; and because I cannot do everything, I will not refuse to do something that I can do.*

These words best embody the personal, intimate feelings all Americans should hold moving forward in 2020. For individuals to understand something that is not part of their everyday reality, they must start small—personal—with an intensity that can only be understood and processed at an individual level first. And then, maybe then, as individuals practice exercising agency—not only self-control or discipline, but proactively, a deliberate improvement upon thoughts, attitudes, and behaviors—can it expand into some macro or broader societal movement that genuinely drives change across races and bridges chasms of mistrust.

For many white individuals, there is a feeling of helplessness on such a topic as a race. The issue is too complicated, too large, too connected to vices, half-truths and stereotypes passed down through generations *and driven further asunder by our partisan media poisoning the well.* To view someone of a different color differently is natural to *any* person. And then to ask them to think outside of that mindset—inculcated nearly every day since birth—is a herculean task. Many of us do not know where to start or whom to start with. Self-examination only takes one so far.

As Albert Einstein explained, "We cannot solve problems by using the same kind of thinking we used when we created them." And since many whites are not deliberately exposed to thinking outside of their tribal framework, the task of imagining a solution to racism becomes all but impossible, especially with the onslaught and fear they have of violent riots in the name of Black Lives Matter. The violent reaction in these instances tends to betray the just cause underlying the outward display of frustration. Trying to make a point in this manner is no different from draining the water from a fish's bowl to teach him he is a fish, when we are all fish living in the same bowl you just drained the water from.

So, what happens? Whites retreat into the safety and regresses of the common culture, erected all around them through predominantly white constructs. There is no need to directly address "whiteness" in a homogenized cultural façade in which "white" is synonymous with "human." One reinforces the other, or at least provides enough sanctuary that whites no longer need to process and decide how they, collectively, should respond when they witness such heinous disregard for their fellow man.

Oh, deep down, they know oppression and injustice are wrong. They may shade it with different grays and fluster over situational moralities, but they know. Yet, to ask white individuals to collectively gather and stand up against something they truly do not fully understand is so alien, so gigantic in its thinking, so radical in its design, there is an arresting trepidation that often leads to inaction. Wait it out . . . this, too, shall pass . . . things will return to "normal" soon enough.

However, the "normal" is what we as a society—persons

of all colors and hues—must push back against, especially for whites. And yet that can only begin at the individual level. And it starts with the solemn recognition that yes, I can stand for change in my own heart and mind, and that can spread to my home, my workplace, my house of worship, my social gatherings, everywhere. This change must occur on both sides simultaneously before we can ever meet in the middle. A cultural change must occur before we can heal as a societal whole.

Edward Hale put his finger on something, and he may not have even known how impactful that could be. Individually, with limits, I can make a difference—not *the* difference, but a difference. Yet, notice what first must occur that Hale does not state but is transparent. The change of that individual comes first with resolution. Hale recognizes that he must first resolve to change before he—or anyone—can stand forth and proclaim that such change will seem inconsequential at first. A resolution is caused by a dilemma. On the one hand, we want to believe that in America, each of us is an individual that should be judged by our actions and not our invidious attributes. On the other hand, we have a long history as a country of espousing those ideals while practicing something entirely different.

Slaves as a "class" were accorded three-fifths "personhood" for enumeration under the original US Constitution. This is an apparent betrayal of the concept of individual liberty for all, equally under the law. Nevertheless, it was done for the sake of political expediency—forming a Union against a bigger enemy while failing to resolve what almost all persons of conscience knew at the time to be an abomination, the enslavement of nearly four million Africans into a nation supposedly founded upon the principles of freedom and liberty.

The unintended consequence of this unresolved tension between tyranny and liberty would come back to bite America in a big way nearly a century later. By that time, the concept of inequality for the three-fifths person had been baked into the social contract. Whites felt that freeing the slaves and making them equal citizens on a par with whites in effect diminished the value of white citizenhood. This unresolved dilemma continues until today, but nowhere near the level to which BLM or other radical groups represent it; they are only taking us backward and hurting all the hard work those such as Rosa Parks demonstrated.

While Black Lives Matter was born from good intention and was a much-needed movement in a society that needed to be recognized and stood up for, over time this pure intent has been hijacked by ill will and taken to the streets with violent mass protest, in most cases with blatant disregard of the masses of peaceful citizens.

The union of America was also hijacked over time, and the purity has moved to politics, so this is not a new issue we are facing. We will always and forever remember Rosa as a hero and an Angel of our time, and all races recognize her as such, but we will not look back in time and see the violence and destruction of the BLM movement and recognize them as heroes of Peace and Unity for our time. If Rosa or MLK or Gandhi, for that matter, would have picked up arms and started in that way, they would not be seen as heroes and heroines of our day; they would just be another tyrant, no different than the abusive police that we all seek to abolish.

However, we delude ourselves if we think the most significant breakdown of race and racial tensions first began with the institutions that man has created. Minneapolis has some of the most progressive anti-brutality policies in place—launched by individuals who themselves were once protesters challenging police oppression—and yet Derek Chauvin still kneeled on a neck without hesitation. Was his act of depravity the result of an institutional failure, or was it merely an individual failure? Are we launching a complete upheaval because of a few corrupt cops grossly and carelessly misusing power, or is there still a hugely significant systemic race problem? At what point does individual human agency account for the outcomes we seek as a society writ large? At what point do we look in the mirror and see the reflection of our society in each one of ourselves and stop blaming others for our darkness? Only then can we face our fears and change our country's behaviors, starting with the man in the mirror.

IV. Don't Take a Knee: Show Empathy Even If You Disagree on Tactics

The controversy surrounding San Francisco 49ers quarterback Colin Kaepernick, who decided to kneel instead of stand during the singing of the national anthem before games, represents, for some, a gross violation of a sacred place. In many ways, sports stars and entertainers transcend America's social dynamics, and for some, introducing politics into the equation sullies what some see as a pure distillation of what it means to be America. Michael Jordan is considered a god among many, his racial identity all but forgotten amidst his towering legend. Tiger Woods—at least before his fall from grace—was viewed in the same light by many.

Sports stars enjoy the lofty, if somewhat precarious, esteem of being those in whom we invest our collective fantasies about our most powerful achievements. Part of what needs to be seen around this action of kneeling is that yet again we give it more power than it should necessarily deserve, because we as humans in our current state must come up with something to be offended by instead of just seeing the action as one man's simple show of free will. Some of the things that are occurring in our nation are demonstrative and there are laws against these actions that are not being punished, and then there are others such as kneeling that should simply be accepted as an act of individuality, not an act of defiance, because of our opinion that limits another man's freedoms.

Opinions are a freedom as well, but it is our opinions of these idolized legends that create war over how we see things and feel that they should have been done. We must resort to researching to understand before we judge any situation; nothing is as it seems. We crucify these idolized leaders when they don't fit in our box of perception, as if we have no hidden darkness of our own, and on the very same hand, we follow their lead into a battle in which we fail to take the time to even understand what we are fighting for. We are just following like sheep to the slaughter.

And when the lights come on in the stadium for the Monday night game, the last thing anyone wants to talk about are the things that divide us (aside from our favorite teams, obviously). And yet, even on this stage, at the ultimate moment of the crowning of the American gladiator—politics somehow creeps in, and in an instant an innocent place of gathering becomes a stadium-sized stage for division and propaganda.

Beyoncé's halftime show during Super Bowl 50 in 2016 was a tour-de-force of pop performance; she did not disappoint in terms of her talent and choreography. But she also chose the platform to deliver a somewhat coded message about the struggle between police and the black community—ending her show with dancers dressed in Black Panther-looking regalia, giving what was perceived to be a military salute. The most interesting part of this is how few people picked up on it and yet she is a leader in our community on a grand scale. One can only imagine how large that could become when it's supported as you see with BLM.

"Wait up a minute," many people muttered from their couches in front of the TV after her show, "Did my eyes deceive me? Has Beyoncé actually desecrated the holiest day of the sports year by promoting a radical political agenda?" There were two principal lines of argument that seemed to generate most of the controversy. The first was that Beyoncé chose the side of Black Lives Matter over police officers and thereby disrespected officers who have laid down their lives to uphold the law; not to mention many officers who were actively involved in providing security for the very venue in which Beyoncé chose to express her allegedly "anti-cop" views. Others took the exact opposite position, that by co-opting the symbolism and imagery of the Black Panthers within a pop performance, Beyoncé belittled the black power movement and exploited the civil rights struggle for commercial gain.

I implore you to ask yourselves, how is it that we only see what is seemingly negative? How have we become so pro- grammed in this country that we permit negativity to over- shadow all the massive amount of good that is done in society by incredible citizens? Unfortunately, the good that occurs is more commonly overlooked and ignored because it doesn't cause drama that the media and certain leaders, namely those who traffic in race grievance politics, can sell and use to divide us. In other words, we've allowed these entities and so-called leaders to turn many of us into being in a perpetual state of grievance.

Whether one fell on one side or the other of the argument, both sides seemed to agree that by injecting politics into a pub- lic sporting event, Beyoncé unfairly ambushed an unsuspect- ing public. As with the actions of Colin Kaepernick, or Tommy Smith and John Carlos who raised their fists in protest while on the medal stand at the 1968 Olympics, public outcry over Beyoncé's actions seemed to center on the propriety of the place of protest rather than the merits of their political agenda.

And for many, the actions of Beyoncé, Kaepernick, and

others really begs the question of whether a sporting event is the proper venue for voicing political views. And look, this is a sports venue that holds 75,000 people, and they see this as a one-night stand. Then, we go home and allow the media to bombard our two most vulnerable entrances to our Soul, our eyes and our ears, with nothing more than over-exaggerated, one-sided propaganda that lines their pockets. These sports or entertainment icons are a drop in the bucket compared to big media that is dishonest or has agendas in their productions.

But the fact remains, they are tempting places. After all, those are often some of the most televised moments where those with a message can capture the attention of millions of Americans, but is that what people want and need? Some may say there is never a right time, while others will argue sporting events and concerts are the most optimum time to get a symbolic message across. During the Baltimore riots in April 2013, protesters showed up outside the Orioles baseball stadium and confronted exiting fans in a tense standoff that ultimately resulted in the cancellation of a game.

The act of using the sports arena as a political platform offended many, more than even the property damage that occurred in other parts of the city at the hands of the rioters. Two days later, due to public safety concerns, the public was banned from attending, and the Orioles played to an empty stadium. This was perhaps the last straw for many. What in the world did baseball fans have to do with the social plight of inner-city Baltimore residents? The answer is absolutely nothing—this was nothing more than an act of terrorism that was quickly forgotten because there was no real cause to stand for.

But that, quite ironically, may be the point. When we take on our different identities—husband, mother, coworker, sports fan—we do not leave all our other identities at the door. When we identify with an ideal, it becomes awfully hard to stay open to other ideas or perceptions. One must consciously work to maintain an open mind or differences will result in judgment and ultimately division. To some poor protestors, the stadium and the fans represented a physical manifestation of the mainstream political establishment they were hell-bent on challenging. However, one flaw in that line of thinking is that many of the patrons of sporting events are hardworking people, too, who just want a few hours to escape the normal grind of life's uncertainties.

It's sad to say but those who are in fight or flight mode see anything that they perceive as better than their current position as the enemy, and they are closed to any other perception until enough pain has been incurred to change their minds. But there may also have been a tinge of envy involved too; as if the protesters were saying, "Why should you get to enjoy your fantasy pastime in peace and safety, while we have to be confronted with hard realities on the streets?"

On the other hand, the fact that the US military uses sporting events as a recruiting tool proves their political value in ways that have now become so embedded in our national consciousness that we are not always aware of them. We have become blindly accepting, over time, of war, as well as of propaganda. To the police and military, it is assumed that professional sports and patriotic displays go hand in hand. The point here is that by affirming traditions such as the military flyover and standing for the national anthem, sports has long been a venue for politics—and in fact, they are by default a political platform.

It is critically important that we acknowledge that politics and political voice are important for all sides in this debate. If we could all dictate what said debate should look like, it removes the necessity for debate in the first place. One problem with most people is that they like comfort because comfort permits us to overlook or ignore things that we might otherwise be forced to reconcile with. Our current culture is so consumed with comfort that work has even come to be seen as an annoyance. We must get across to our children and their children that life starts at the edge of comfort. This ideal of comfort is also destroying our country. We have so many households where fathers sit on the couch all day and expect the check from the government to take care of the family they have created, and it causes them to feel insignificant. Yet they are the first to help deface statues of heroes that formed this country or burn a police car to get a false sense of significance and a rush of endorphins that they can't get from sitting on their couch doing nothing to advance themselves or their family all day every day.

It is somewhat ironic that we are now facing rebellion and strife; we are begging for civil demonstrations in the place of rioting and looting. And yet, just a few short years ago, even peaceful demonstrations were a bridge too far along the road to political correctness. In hindsight, wasn't Kaepernick's and Beyoncé's "virtue symbology" a far milder reminder than the virtue-bashing occurring on the streets of America today? Recall the Boston Tea Party. If the British had heeded the warning and curtailed their repressive taxes and allowed the colonists to have a political voice, we might never have had an American Revolution and, for better or worse, remained until today a British colony.

Yet, when you look at this instance, there was real cause that was fought for with dignity and under leaders who stood for solid values. This is a major piece of the puzzle we are missing today, leaders that are congruent in all areas of their life and that align with the true need of the people, even if it's tough love saying NO!

Others may beg to differ. In 2003, at the height of their mega-stardom, country music band the Dixie Chicks, now known as the Chicks, stood in front of a crowd in England and uttered the simple words:

"Just so you know, we're on the good side with y'all. We do not want this war, this violence, and we're ashamed that the president of the United States is from Texas."

Here we are dealing with a fine point. The country was on edge and had just invaded Iraq in the aftermath of the devastating terrorist attack on America on 9/11. The country music industry exploded in indignation at their comments, and the Chicks were blacklisted from radio for almost ten years. Their political statement was viewed as unpatriotic, not merely because they had criticized President Bush, but because they had done so during a war.

The Chicks were eventually welcomed back into the fold— but not through the door of country music from which they exited the stage. Their comeback album *Taking the Long Way* won the 2007 Grammy Awards for Album of the Year, Record of the Year, and Song of the Year. One wonders whether their red carpet Hollywood welcome was due to the fact that they had been forgiven their sacrilege, or whether their views were ultimately vindicated by what had by that time become a widely unpopular war in the Middle East.

Yet here again, let's ask another question. Let's pretend that instead of the devastation of thousands of lives and families in an unthinkable act, the Middle East had just dropped 50,000 highly trained soldiers in Texas who raided the city that the Chicks lived in and took their family members captive. Do you think they would have shamed the president for acting, or at that point would they have been an advocate of war? See, this is free-thinking, it is not about selfish thinking; it's about selfless thinking and putting yourself in the other person's shoes for just a single moment, then making a decision on how you would act. We all deserve this simple respect.

The point remains a fundamental one, though. It is often not the underlying political issue that people find most disconcerting about the contentious mixture of sports, entertainment, and politics. The issue is that many fans come to the arena for the express purposes of escaping troubling issues and being entertained for a while. Our desire for instant relief or gratification as a society is part of the reason we find ourselves in this internal cultural battle. Everyone is so accustomed to getting their fix from external circumstances that we fail to look inward for lasting change. At a certain point, repeated violations of sacred spaces of gathering, such as the coliseum or stadium, lose their shock value and can end up causing more harm to their cause than help.

Especially in the fact that they not only support, but are designed for competition. In the arena there is no partisanship; it is one-sided, and that is always the home side. BLM was designed from a place of pure intention to advance society, yet it has turned into another place of seeing one another as opposites—in opposition to the other's systems of belief, and therefore, they (the opposition) are the enemy and must be regarded as such.

Athletes and entertainers using their enormous platforms to get involved in the cultural and political problems plaguing our society is not a new phenomenon. Baseball great Jackie Robinson, who was the first African American to play in the major leagues, used his platform both on and off the baseball field. After retiring from the sport in 1957, Jackie became vice president at the Chock Full O' Nuts coffee company.

During his time at the company, Robinson used his platform and position to encourage the Republican Party to appeal to black people. He debated civil rights with Presidents Kennedy, Johnson, and Nixon and even had public disagreements with Malcolm X and Rev. Dr. Martin L. King Jr. Like many of the stars today, Robinson never shied away from using his platform to focus on the issues he deemed important. Robinson understood the value of hard work to build something worth fighting for. He realized that Chock Full O' Nuts was his real, world-changing empire in a country that was built on industry and capitalism that supported and employed its communities. These are the values that we seek today, and we will not find them in violence and destruction.

There's also the godfather of soul, James Brown, who wrote politically charged songs such as "Say It Loud (I'm Black and I'm Proud)." Brown performed his songs at civil rights demonstrations and used his platform to raise awareness about racial inequities of that time. Please understand, though, there was still a very heavy influence of racism back then. The children who are acting out on our streets today have no idea of what Jackie Robinson and James Brown and many other icons went through to become great black leaders of their time.

The *true* racial opposition that they faced would have caused these spoiled children looting our streets to have a standing heart attack. The distance this country has traveled since that time is equivalent to crossing galaxies in a canoe. James Brown further engulfed himself into politics with his stay-in-school song "Don't Be a Drop-Out," which encouraged young African Americans to stay in school to complete their education.

Despite his celebrity, Brown's activism wasn't well received by all African Americans. After he endorsed Vice President Hubert Humphrey for president, he was called an "Uncle Tom" and his critics referred to him as "Sold Brother No. 1." Yet I assure you that had Brown acted out in the way we see today with the riots in our streets and the destruction of our country and business, both white and black owned, there would have been zero progress made in the furthering of the message that Brown is still influencing today with resounding freedom for all in the entire country.

Beyoncé and Kaepernick aren't and won't be the first athlete and performer to use their platforms to dive into politics. After all, they are people too and though we expect them to focus on what we come to love them for, we shouldn't be surprised when they take positions on issues we may disagree with them on. Perhaps we should love them for being good athletes and performers while being able to respectfully disagree with their politics, because at the end of the day, you'll never agree with anyone one hundred percent of the time on anything, regardless of how much you love them.

In September 2016, the superintendent of schools in the OK Conference in Western Michigan banned the presentation of the Betsy Ross American flag and chants by students and fans of "USA" during high school sports games because they were supposedly offensive symbols of racial hatred. Many people have been left scratching their heads at this seemingly bizarre display of political correctness and wondering, quite appropriately: since when did patriotism and nationalism become the new "N-word"?

We have not only become weak regarding the word "offensive," we have embraced the essence of a coward, who would rather seek to dismiss challenging dialogue than face any of it at all with an actual opinion on the subject that can be backed up with experience and research. We have become a society of parrots that would rather fall in line and wear a mask and gloves because we were told to, instead of researching the issue and searching for our own true opinion of the issue, then speaking out on it. There was a day when we needed to go to war for these issues, but we have long evolved from that. Look around. Very few individuals want to wage war anymore. We can be a peaceful society at this point.

School superintendent Dan Behm initially defended the students' activities, citing an annual display of the colors red, white, and blue in conjunction with the schools' commemoration of the 9/11 terrorist attacks; sounds innocuous enough. Some students, however, also displayed Donald Trump campaign flags alongside their American flags, obviously promoting a partisan political agenda that extended beyond a display of patriotism. Every display of patriotism, whether raising a flag or burning one, should be honored in this country founded on freedom, as long as it's done in peace and does not harm another. But in the event that it physically harms another human being, there will be war and that is also what freedom was founded on.

In a letter to the school after the event, Behm expressed as much, stating, "Injecting partisan politics into a community football game and into a commemoration of the events of September 11th is inappropriate." And it would have been fine if the comment ended there. But he continued: "Parading our current United States flag in a manner that is inconsistent with proper etiquette is disrespectful to all who have served our nation. And, to wave a historical version of our flag, that to some symbolizes exclusion and hate, injects hostility and confusion to an event where no one intended to do so."

Here we see the perfect execution of power on a simple opinion when a display of patriotism was done in peace. No individual should be allowed to deny any human being a display of opinion in the United States of America. If we continue down this path, we would end up having to change the entire name of the Country we deeply Love, to reflect the socialism that we will embrace in its place.

Commenters on the popular local news website M-Live

found the accusation to be unfair. "This whole PC thing has gotten way out of hand," said one commenter. "Why is it acceptable to proudly wear a Black Lives Matter T-shirt, and not our country's flag?" We have created a government that has done *everything* you can imagine to side with minorities of all races, giving them every possible head start you could think of. I have seen the number of walls that have been removed to allow the so-called "disenfranchised" to be not only allowed, but empowered to succeed in this country.

If these programs had been around fifty years ago, there would be more black billionaire leaders than you could count, but there weren't. But you know what? There are now, and no one is taking the time to even look! They want it placed in front of their face, the pen placed in their hand and their hand held and another human to do it all for them. I don't know about you but that is not how I built my empire, and I cringe to think that this could be the future of our country catering to these entitled babies—but truly we are to blame—both white and black. We have not paid attention to the rearing of our children and in this lies the root of this issue. In the early 1900s family was everything. Family values mattered. Disrespect was punished, not by the police, but by the family.

My white and black brothers and sisters, this is where we can all look in the mirror and say we have failed. For this we must take responsibility, how we do this, this is the question and I beg of you to ask this of yourself as I will myself. God as my witness, I will do my best to right this sinking ship we blew holes in.

The concern we must have about where we're headed should be grave because we are openly embracing a culture that even former President Barack Obama lamented when he stated, "this idea of purity and you're never compromised, and you're always politically 'woke' and all that stuff. You should get over that quickly. The world is a mess, there are ambiguities. People who do good stuff have flaws. People who you are fighting may love their kids. And share certain things with you." Life isn't one great utopia, it's hard, it's challenging, and to paint a rosy picture for our kids sets them up for failure when they're forced to deal with the harsh realities of life.

Schools are entities that exist to expand our young people's minds, to challenge them on what they believe. Our public schools were originally built back in the days of industry, they were building factories, and they needed workers educated enough to hire and keep the country's industries moving forward. There was a time for this, and it was called the Industrial Revolution. We have evolved so much, and we seem to have forgotten what we came through and the foundation that was laid, but there are parts of that foundation that *must* evolve, and one of them is our school system. America's school system is far behind the times and needs a total reform—this too I will stand behind—our children need family and they need education in a new way for a new future.

It makes sense, of course, that schools should regulate the display of banners, symbols, and even words that might be considered inflammatory and divisive. It would be foolish to display everyone's opinion of how life should be depicted, yet I assure you that is where we are headed, a flag to display each of the seven billion different individual opinions on the earth.

After all, matters of school safety and promoting an environment conducive to learning must always be balanced against the free speech rights of students and other members of the school community. Symbols that may in some contexts seem perfectly benign may in others be used to confront and divide people. But to imply that an original version of the American flag automatically injects hate and hostility seems a bit of a stretch. This stretch is a simple example of what is happening in America today; at one point it's a stretch of opinion and then the next thing you know it's the destruction and defacing of monumental statues of the heroes who formed this nation.

To many people, the Betsy Ross flag celebrates the American Revolution and the genesis of the American Constitution. In recent years it has been used as a symbol of resistance to globalism and the need for a restoration of constitutional principles. Flown next to a Trump banner, it may serve to reinforce the ideology of maintaining America's sovereign rights, especially given Trump's America-first philosophy. And for some, it instills a heightened level of love of our country amidst a more globally interconnected world, where globalism has come to dominate the will of nations, and Trump, for good or bad, is for many the last stand to preserving some of the greatest aspects of American idealism.

Many Americans fail to even know or understand where this flag was born or the freedom and passion that it originated from, yet they will persecute it because they would rather follow a fool and feel significant than follow freedom and have to find themselves in it.

But the bigger problem with preempting almost all political expression—even in a school setting—is that doing so tends to suppress the legitimate voices of Americans. Continuing to suppress freedom of expression in this way may lead to frustration and inspire potentially less constructive ways of voicing social discontent. We do not ever want to get to the point where people are resorting to less positive means of expression. The war of words may be intense, but it is highly preferable to a war of physical violence. The ability to have robust debate about complicated issues goes to the core of who we are as a democratic republic. Our nation wasn't built on giving up, which underscores a certain aspect that goes to the very core of our republic, which was built on maintaining the ability to have healthy debate and dialogue on tough issues in search of honest answers and solutions.

This episode provides yet another indication that *ex uno plures* (from one unified nation, a thousand splintered tribes) is replacing *e pluribus unum* as a lingua franca in political discourse; sometimes imagined slights are given just as much credence as actual insults. When we reach the point that we cry wolf over every imagined instance of offense, it makes real cries of offense and harm less effective. No one can hear them through the noise. Let's not risk throwing out the baby with the bathwater by over-regulating free speech; we have already given up enough freedom as it is, where will this stop?

Free speech isn't always comfortable, we're not going to always like it, but it is necessary. Debates must be won through dialogue and the exchange of ideas, and if someone has ideas that are so awful that you want to cringe, we make those arguments when we argue through our logic by debate, but we can't debate in a world that denies the freedom of speech.

There is an additional lesson to be learned here. We need to be more tolerant of each other—wait though, we actually must eliminate tolerance and replace it with acceptance of one another with no predisposed attachment to a desired outcome. In this gift of freedom to one another we will truly find the freedom that we are seeking; one must be willing to give what he seeks so that he can see himself as the Source. While no one is demanding you kneel along with athletes—recall that the man who advised Kaepernick to kneel in the first place was a decorated war veteran who chooses to stand—we should certainly attempt to empathize with the underlying reasons for the expression, and not merely take umbrage with the way it is communicated. We must seek to understand before we can possibly ask to be understood.

We are slowly reaching a point where we're losing sight of the underlying grievances that are being protested because we don't like the optics, but as I noted earlier, what exactly is the proper way to protest? Kaepernick, Beyoncé, and others have done so symbolically and peacefully, and many condemned them. But now we're seeing looting and rioting in our streets, and this has become the end result of peaceful but uncomfortable protesting. So the question we must ask ourselves is what we are doing as individuals to help heal our national divide, because at the end of the day, every last one of us is only responsible for the self, and as hard as it may be to hear, the self is reflected in the whole.

So then we must challenge ourselves to be a part of the solution, and being a part of the solution is acknowledging that perhaps there are some underlying problems that exist and require putting forth the work to better ourselves, because if we can work to do that, we can work to heal the problems that have so incessantly divided us.

We are really treading on dangerous ground when the very rituals we use to celebrate national unity become characterized by some as symbols of division. What's next? Will the national anthem itself be banned because someone is offended by its revolutionary call to arms? In fact, that would have seemed absurd even three years ago, but amidst the current crisis, that is just what is happening, Liana Morales, a graduating senior at the Urban Assembly School for the Performing Arts in New York, refused to sing the national anthem at her graduation[1], but

---

1   https://www.wsj.com/articles/high-school-graduation-singer-refuses-to-sing-star-spangled-banner-11592830800

instead chose to sing the "black national anthem," "Lift Ev'ry Voice and Sing." If this was done from a place of pure unbiased love for the country, then I would be okay with it, but we can all feel that this is not true, and until it is true, we will stand divided and at war with a race that is divided by racism, a completely made-up concept that simply shows how unevolved we are, and we are allowing the law of polarity to define us.

When it comes to American traditions, African American rituals, Confederate monuments, we should respect all of them, even if we do not agree on the meaning of the expression. There's a definite upside to all this. We can be proud of our young folks who are learning about their history and gaining a sense of civic pride. These are exactly the type of activities that lead to informed citizens exercising their constitutional rights. We may be going too far in regulating imperfect speech, at the cost of producing citizens who are afraid to think for themselves. And one of the fundamental values that we share as Americans is the ability to disagree with the speech, yet staunchly uphold the right to speak freely. In fact, this may be the only real glue holding the ship together at this point, and I don't need to tell you that if the glue gets too thin, the whole ship will sink.

Free speech does not exist, it never has, and it never will. The promise of America was never to have perfect speech, but free speech, and that means there will be speech you dislike—but it gives you the opportunity to challenge that which you dislike, and it also gives the right to war when lives are threatened or taken because of your opinion. So I urge you to reconsider how we rally for our opinion. Are we *being* the change we want to see, or are we fighting our greatest enemy and blaming everyone else because we are too afraid to acknowledge that the Enemy we are afraid to fight is the Self looking back at us in the Mirror?

V. We're All in This Together: Your Voice Needs to Be Heard, Too

It is tempting to tell ourselves that we do not have a problem; that things will eventually blow over. Staying silent is not a sign of consent but merely prudence. But remember, as Aristotle taught us, virtue is a means. The virtue of courage is the difference between cowardice and foolhardiness. Aristotelian moral courage teaches us not to be too rash or too fearful, which requires us to intellectually look at the intrinsic value of a claim and pursue its normative value. However, that is seldom the case, as a great many men and women are all too willing to make a claim with no basis and those judging the claim are willing to cast judgment without serious investigation. In essence, both groups rule each other out. In his 2011 book *The Inquiring Mind*, Jason Baehr likewise argues that intellectual courage is best construed as a disposition to respond well to threats to one's epistemic well-being.

As we discussed earlier in this book, no one is advocating you go out in the streets and light police vehicles afire; no one is advocating looting or destroying private property or public monuments. No one is saying you have to take a knee. However, you have to take a stand, because at the end of the day, this affects all of us. You take a stand because you understand this affects your community. It affects your children. This issue is not going away. The longer you believe it is going to blow over, the longer the feelings of distress will last.

We as a society cannot wish these problems away, nor can we just hope that they organically improve because while nature heals, it alters and changes in the process and that requires effort and work. We cannot go to bed hoping these problems are a nightmare that only exists during our deepest levels of sleep because once you are awakened, you'll soon realize it was never just a dream, but the harsh reality that you'll never be able to escape. Therefore, it leads us all to face the harsh reality that if it is inescapable, we are left with only one final solution and that is to tackle the problem head-on.

We have reached a pinnacle moment in our society where we need to have voices of moral conscience speaking up, but we must also recognize that those good voices, those voices that seek to be a light in the dark, may not agree on all things. That's okay as long as there is shared agreement on the problem at hand, and I for one believe that there is. I know that Americans of every race and creed cry out for a day when we can move beyond race. I know that men and women of conscience hope for and are willing to work for a society where the next generations and generations unborn know nothing of a society that judges based on race and only know of a society that judges based on the character and moral and ethical system that guides a person and their actions. It is not idealistic to seek to work toward that goal because it is a noble and honorable one.

One way of reframing our perspective about the unrest and violence we see in our streets is that it is just energy. It is windy. It is a storm. However, as any good sailor knows, a strong wind is a good wind, as long as you know how to set your sail. So, rather than waiting for this to blow over, we want to orient our sails in a way that we use the wind to blow us toward our destination. When reframed as merely energy or "wind," we do not attach as much value or judgment to the nature of the wind. It is not good energy or bad energy; it is not a foul or fair wind. It is just wind. We can use it to our advantage.

Once we have become energy-agnostic, wind-neutral, we can begin to see things for what they really are. We are not experiencing the end of America. The people rioting in the streets are not some sinister group of anarchists. They are your neighbors. They have been cooped up in the house for six months, and they are anxious. They are fearful, or they are overly exuberant. They need to be offered a more constructive way to dissipate the pent-up energy. If you have courage, you will not be scared away by them. You will embrace this as a wonderful opportunity to become a better person yourself; to refine your character. To become a leader in your community and the wider world.

So we have to commit at this point to shed ourselves of all cynicism and ambivalence. We are not going to make progress by trying to both cower and advance at once—we have to make a choice. We have to commit ourselves to moving forward, giving voice to our concerns, engaging in constructive dialogue with others, and being willing to have hard conversations. There is no more room to say to yourself, "Hey, I am not political." It is not someone else's job. There is no one better suited to speak up than you are because at the end of the day you are only responsible for the self because you can only control your own actions. While some may say it's someone else's job or I'll just wait, we must ask ourselves: what is it that we're waiting for? What if that someone else never appears, then what?

It is time to stop deluding ourselves into believing that we can opt out of participating in the grand project of making our nation a more perfect union. There is no space for apathy or rationalizing our fears because fear is like a cancer—it will consume everything in its path until there is nothing left. By failing to voice our objections, we are not avoiding wrongdoing; we are directly promoting it. Evil and injustice thrive amidst the silence of good people. Just ask the folks of Nazi Germany. No doubt the Germans are a good and noble folk. How could such a vicious scourge like Hitler have arisen among such an educated and cosmopolitan society as early twentieth-century Germany? Certainly there were myriad factors, including a declining economy and war reparations leading to massive unemployment. However, those stresses, the uncertainty of poverty or dislocation, should not be used as an excuse to forsake our values. In fact, times of trouble are when we need to adhere even more closely to them. We need to speak up for justice, freedom, and equality as if all of our lives really matter.

When we abandon our fellow citizens, who have taken to the streets begging for help, we are committing a new injustice by ignoring them or condemning them. They need our voice, along with their own, to make lasting political and social change in this country. It does us no good at the end of the day to merely rest on our laurels and point to the fantastic success we have had in the past, if we are not today willing to take up the mantle— the same mantle our forefathers took up in standing against the cruel tyrannies of the British crown—and affirm the rights of all of our countrymen and women under the Constitution and just laws of our country.

As the famous Greek orator Pericles once said, "One person's disengagement is untenable unless bolstered by someone else's commitment." If you decide to opt out, you are diminishing the work of the folks who are opting in. You are dead weight. You are free riding at a time when we should all be asking what

more we can do for our country. That does not sound courageous, and it certainly is not wise.

The phrase "we are all in this together" has been debated
in almost all corners of the American political spectrum amidst
the rise of the COVID-19 pandemic. Some have used the term
to call for a national conversation around much-needed priorities. Some have used it as a rallying cry for a socialist revolution.
But others have seen it in its most elevated light—an acknowl-
edgment that our neighbors, our friends, our countrymen and
women are our allies, not our enemies. Our essential workers,
including temporary and seasonal immigrants (who come here
legally), are in this with us. We want our economies to thrive,
to have fresh fruit and veggies delivered to our table, yet we do
not speak up for the migrant farmer or the worker at the meat-
packing plants? We complain about the economy being slow to
reopen, yet we are not insisting frontline workers such as the
grocery store clerk or the delivery driver get hazard pay?

We do not need to be acolytes of a single party to be a voice
for justice, but we do need to be sons and daughters of liberty.
Equality under the law, social justice, diversity, and prosperity are themselves the progeny of liberty. It is the freedom that
throughout the ages has lifted people from abject poverty, allowed
for education, prosperity, the emergence of a middle class, and
movement over time from ignorance to erudition, from scarcity
to abundance. The task at hand, then, is the expansion of liberty
to include all people without hesitation or qualification warmly. It
is, as President Lincoln said at Gettysburg, "for us the living . . . to
be dedicated here to the unfinished work . . ." Our labor continues
as long as any of our citizens are denied the full embrace of liberty.
This, then, becomes our litmus test. Any act of government that
expands liberty should enjoy our support, while those that undermine it deserve our opposition. Raising taxes, increased burden

of regulation, redlining in banking or real estate all diminish liberty.

Enterprise zones, choice in education, and reasonable access to revenue for establishing businesses all expand freedom. Here careful scrutiny is needed. In general, as the government expands, liberty contracts. Like all Americans, African Americans will flourish not by dint of government largesse but by participating without hindrance in a free and open market. The free enterprise system is the greatest system known to man and has lifted more men, women, and children out of poverty than any other program known to man. One merely needs to look at countries that were once restricted, such as India or parts of Asia, that completely or partially opened up their economies to the capitalist system. They have seen a decrease in poverty, an increase in their living conditions, an increase in wage earnings—their overall life improvements have increased exceptionally. We in the United States should know this better than any other country in the world—after all, look at what capitalism has done for our once agrarian society, that became an industrial juggernaut, to where we are now, dominating the globe in practically every sector. It was capitalism that gave us that advantage and it will be capitalism that continues to give advantages to anyone who is willing to put in the hard work to earn it. This economic system is what will also continue to elevate the most vulnerable in our society by giving them an opportunity to build sustainable wealth that can be passed down to generations.

The system of free exchange and voluntary cooperation is essential for rebuilding and uplifting our hardest-hit communities for rural and urban Americans, including poor blacks, whites, and Hispanics. Most people don't want a handout; most want a hand up and a fair opportunity coupled with access to make their dreams a reality. America can't promise that everyone will be successful, but we can ensure that everyone has the same access and opportunities to the resources necessary to create that success, whatever it is for the individual.

The government needs to provide safety, security, and a civil atmosphere for conducting business. The people themselves will then pursue and achieve their prosperity. When seen through this lens of liberty, the older approaches of expanding government presence through ambitious social programs will have an enfeebling effect and undermine individual sovereignty. President Lincoln's unfinished work is at this moment ours. Expand liberty and allow for the creation of prosperity and its fruits. Our ambition is "that this nation shall have a new birth of freedom and that government of the people, by the people, for the people, shall not perish from the earth."

We do not have to toe a party line on race in order to be a voice for justice. In fact, that is the opposite of what we should be doing. We need people with courage, those who are unafraid of speaking the truth free of the political correctness that has handicapped our society and disabled our ability to speak the truth about the realities as we see them. Political parties have become a part of the problem as their sole purpose is to get and retain power by any means necessary, and sometimes that isn't always advantageous to moving the country together as one. But we cannot move forward together if we are divided. Division can become our downfall if we allow it, which is why we must once and for all deal with this original sin.

But we must be a voice for justice. We do not have to virtue-signal to be a force for positive change. But we have to be actually virtuous. And we have to see this as a fight: not just for civil rights, or for African Americans, but for all of our survival. In the past weeks and months, we have seen all the divisiveness, invective, and strife we are capable of. But as good people of conscience, we have to work together to transform that energy into something constructive. And we can do this. We can do it by affirming the simple yet revolutionary proposition that all men and women are created equal. We can do it by shunning discrimination and hatred in all of its forms—and most notably in how such negative attitudes form in our hearts.

All of this internal work and external validation of our highest ideals must stem from a place of deep humility, deep caring, and empathy. We have to commit ourselves to listening, learning, and leading constructive change. However, it can't be temporary change, it can't occur in time to only become back-grounded; it must become permanent, and that is easier said than done. Permanent change requires commitment and con-sistency, and such an operation of sustaining a new modem of operation is only sufficient if we dedicate ourselves to doing it.

However, just as there are men and women of good con-science, there will always be naysayers—those looking to divide, those who don't want to see racial harmony. Those individuals are the greatest threat to America as a whole making sustained progress. These individuals will claim that it is implausible for the magnitude of change that we seek to occur and will attempt to deter us from it. They may even go as far as to say that the thing we're attempting to change can never exist in and of itself. Another method to deny all Americans coming together. But their argument is a flawed illusion that is both dubious and dan-gerous because the United States is built on the idea that we're able to become a better nation tomorrow than we were yesterday or even today.

The United States of America is a country that wasn't built on giving up. It is a country that is built on the idea that our best days are still ahead of us. It is built on the idea that if we work together as a great collective, there isn't anything we cannot do if we commit ourselves to doing it. So I know that the society we can have will be for me and for you what we work toward creating it to be. Think about the things we've gone through as a nation and the considerable progress we've made, from slavery to the Civil War to where we are today. We continue to move forward in the right direction and I believe we are destined to remain doing so.

So then we must say to the skeptics, who believe it is both unrealistic and unreasonable for us to challenge ourselves to continue to craft the more perfect union our founders said we can, that they are wrong and can't obviously understand the history of this great nation. There is a reason that the United States remains that great city shining on a hill. We were yesterday, today, and will forever be in the future a beacon of hope for the rest of the world, because the promise of America is the belief in the human spirit to always live up to its great potential—that which God created in all men, women, and children—and that is to be our best selves.

So then the final question that we must all ask ourselves is can we do better? Do we have a moral obligation to let our voices be heard? I believe the unabashed truth to both questions is simply yes. We need to regain each other's trust in order to truly move forward and claim our highest prize as a nation. Contemporary politics have in many instances stunted our hopes and dreams about the possibilities of what we're capable of as Americans. And the further we seep into this dark boundless hole of emptiness, void of both space and time, we slowly lose a sense of who we are as a society of people born of freedom. We slowly fall into the insufferable category of great empires that once were. This must not become our future; this must not become our destiny.

VI. Why Having Honest Dialogue Is So Difficult (And What to Do about It)

It seems we as a society have come to acknowledge that we need to come together to have a real, honest conversation about race. However, just because we know we need to have this conversation does not necessarily mean that we are actually ready to have it. In order to prepare for this difficult but necessary dialogue, perhaps we can anticipate some of the likely points of contention and frame the discussion around *bringing awareness to this matter.*

First of all, you may ask: what in the world is a black man telling white people what they should be doing to prepare *them* for this conversation about race? After all, if the shoe were on the other foot, would black folks be as accepting of whites' "prescriptions" for how blacks should feel or act toward what they perceive as a deeply personal history of racism in America? The answer is plain: no. But it shouldn't be. You can quickly point to narratives in the media and elsewhere of African Americans, including members of Black Lives Matter, criticizing whites for somehow interfering with the movement for social change by raising their own voices. Please understand the words of individuals such as myself, who earnestly seek change, imploring you to hear not the sound and fury of the mob that seeks to destroy life and property.

But the conversation at times has become so one-sided that it almost misses the point. In fact, one of the BLM movement's ironies is that it seeks to establish that black lives should matter—to whites. It almost goes without saying that BLM is not an inward-facing movement, but in fact, and quite explicitly so, an *outward*-facing one. In other words, when a black person is gunned down by another black person, whether in a criminal situation or domestic incident, or even when a black police officer kills a black suspect, BLM is nowhere to be found. It is usually only when a white police officer (or self-deputized agent of the law, as we saw in the Ahmaud Arbery case) guns down a black person that BLM cries begin.

So, if Black Lives Matter is directed at white America, or the criminal justice system as a whole, why is it that whites are somehow expected not to have an opinion or a point of view on how the system impacts both blacks and whites?

Perhaps it is time to give the unwritten racial rules a rest. Both blacks and whites have contributed to the racial problems in this country, and we are both going to have to acknowledge our share of the responsibility—albeit in different ways—before we can resolve it. While whites may not always understand or even know how blacks feel or think, they can empathize, but blacks must also recognize that by joining radical groups like BLM, we must hold them accountable when they lose the moral high ground and make excuses for violence and destruction. While we understand that we need to change, we should look to enact change within a framework of creative nonviolence, much like Dr. Martin Luther King Jr. and the Southern Christian Leadership Coalition were able to accomplish during the

1960s. Like everyone else in the black community, Dr. King was incensed and outraged by the power structure's stubborn refusal to address black oppression and inequality. But like a true moral leader, he realized that he had to direct the energy of protest into a more constructive set of principles and actions—and so he developed the strategy of creative nonviolence to expose the system for what it was.

While a man does not directly know what it is like for a woman to be pregnant, for example, there are other ways he can gain information (such as reading or listening to actual women describe their experience) and empathize with the feelings of a pregnant woman. We live in a society that has not always treated women fairly—women were denied the right to vote until well into the twentieth century, and in other ways denied education and full participation in the workplace.

But if women had, in righteous indignation, taken to the streets and threatened to burn the country down in order to be heard, they might not have been able to gain the assistance and cooperation of men to enact legislation and implement structures that helped women achieve some of the social and economic parity they clearly enjoy today. The pregnant woman analogy is similar but not the same as the feelings that blacks have about racism vis-à-vis whites, and that again comes down to the fact that whites are direct participants in the relationship and therefore are necessarily aware of some of the dynamics—unlike men.

The instinct to treat whites as mere spectators who should perhaps listen, be quiet, and support from afar denies the reality that whites and blacks are both full participants in the dance of race. I would definitely be willing to listen to a white person's experience and description of the race problem. I would also be open to hearing what that person thought of as possible solutions. In fact, I would welcome an honest dialogue in a setting where people can feel they won't be attacked for voicing their perspectives.

In an environment where open spaces are becoming ever more contentious—with people spilling into the streets, defacing property, toppling monuments and symbols, desecrating and removing flags—finding safe space for dialogue is becoming harder and harder. That is why we need to be proactive about creating safe spaces for dialogue and debate, spaces where we can hash issues out before exposing ideas to the broader social critique that is sure to follow any attempt to lead the real social transformation. We want a space that is free from distraction so that we can strategize and build, parse, burnish, and iterate.

A. Blackface—If It Seems Offensive It Probably Is

On the one hand, there are familiar racial tropes that have been used historically to belittle and stereotype blacks—for example, wearing blackface in public. The issue is somewhat nuanced in that sometimes the wearer intends to depict a "stereotypical" black person in a humiliating way. Other times, the wearer is attempting to wear a costume depicting a specific person whose skin color is darker than theirs. This distinction came to a head when former NBC *Today* host Megyn Kelly argued in a discussion about Halloween that it was okay to dress up in blackface as long as you were actually depicting a character, such as, say, Michael Jackson. "Back when I was a kid, that was okay, as long as you were dressing up as a character," Kelly claimed.

While the media failed to distinguish between blackface—the stereotype—and putting on dark makeup to dress up in costume as a specific character, what was Kelly trying to gain by even introducing the concept? Was it a necessary statement that contained some truth that was so important that she actually "needed" to bring it up at all?

The point here is that an honest conversation about race must start from a place of awareness and empathy. Ignorance is not a defense against offensiveness. Here is where the virtue of prudence shines. If there is no real reason to introduce a subject that, even at best, might be misconstrued, then why do it?

Megyn Kelly further compounded the mistake when other cohosts, sensing her error, attempted to correct her and get her to avoid the subject. "If you think it's offensive, it probably is," said the author and television host Melissa Rivers. "Whatever happened to just manners, and polite society?" But Kelly persisted in attempting to justify her statement by implying that on Halloween, people do all sorts of "offensive" things, like "running around with fake axes coming out of their head."

The problem with this defense should be obvious. If you make a mistake and someone gently reminds you that continuing down this line of dialogue may be offensive to them—it is prudent to stop. This is perhaps hard to do when you truly mean no offense; you may feel confronted or as if your character or integrity is being called into question. But the key here is to respect the other person's boundaries and tread lightly. There is bound to arise a situation in the near future where they may say something you find offensive. If you've already established that bond of trust, you can gently remind them that they would not like to be stereotyped either and affirm your (already established) commitment to respecting their feelings.

B. White Privilege—Don't Be Guilted into Silence

The use of the "white privilege" label is pejorative and designed to communicate that whites have only achieved or succeeded because the "system" is rigged in their favor. This focuses society solely on race and misses the more active, consequential, and intimate factors in an individual's life: e.g., family, faith, education, work experience, neighborhood, etc. The label also misses the reality of many, if not most, whites that have not been "privileged." Further, it ignores the spectacular achievement by people of every race in America, regardless of the hurdles and obstacles they may have faced. The bottom line is that "whites" are not the only people who succeed in America.

Also, the term "white privilege" masks a deeper truism: that we are all privileged to be Americans. Despite our problems, we continue to enjoy the highest standards of living anywhere in the world. We abound in land, sea, air, forest, and wildlife. We have a public and private education system that, if taken advantage of, enables almost anyone with discipline and drive to build a comfortable life for themselves. Let us not mess that up by talking about this or that group having special privileges. Instead, our approach to dialogue should focus on how we can all enjoy and preserve and even enhance the level of privilege we all can enjoy as citizens of this great land.

Like other racially charged labels—thug, welfare mom, urban crime, etc.—phrases like "white privilege" sound like yet another awful racial epithet used to accuse and diminish another person's humanity. It adds heat to any discussion, but no light. It is a step backward in our nation's long and fraught march to a colorblind society. We are still making progress along that road, of course, but using racial monikers only hinders progress and stifles open discussion. It drives people to their respective "racial" corners, which is not helpful if what we are seeking is to create an avenue for constructive dialogue leading to societal transformation. The truth is that as long as anyone of any race or ethnicity is looking for significance outside of themselves, they will remain in that racial corner. For some, this is comforting because it gives them an excuse to remain marginalized and nonproductive.

Furthermore, by accepting this kind of labeling, you are accepting the status quo—that whites automatically have advantages denied to blacks and others. However, if we are trying to change that—to become a more open and inclusive society—we have to come to terms that enable us to cast off the tribal labels and view each other as individuals with a unique set of gifts endowed by our creator. We must step up in Unity and Responsibility to raise a new generation of freethinking individuals that have been led into knowledge and are experiencing the wisdom of Unity. If we are steadfast in practicing this, the generational curse of racism will be broken.

The way to deal with this accusation—that somehow merely because of your skin color you have an unfair privilege in life—is to gently ask the person you are speaking with whether he or she would prefer to be judged on an individual basis, or purely as a class or group? Would they like for people to assume things about them based on stereotypes, or should someone get to know them before making such an assumption? After all, you are being asked to withhold judgment and get to know people based on their actual identity. Why should you not expect the same in return? Remember, an essential element of this experiment is to embody the change we desire to see in the outer world.

C. Shun the N-Word

It should go without saying, but the N-word should not be used in any conversation. Unfortunately, many people seem to need to have that explicitly stated. No, it is not okay if you are merely parroting some rap lyrics. It is not okay because black people also use the N-word among themselves. It is not okay because you used an "a" ending rather than an "er" ending. It should bear repeating that even white rappers like Eminem, who are deeply accepted and loved within black urban culture, never use the N-word!

Of course, Eminem may be guilty of a whole host of other problems—glorifying drugs, violence, and misogyny, among other issues. However, he is very conscientious about never using the N-word, even when he is in a room full of black folks who toss it around casually. In this case, and in this case alone, follow Eminem's lead. I have white brothers who have casual civil conversations with my black brothers and who get the N-word tossed around multiple times in a one-minute conversation. Now we must ask ourselves what environment was this child raised in that would cause him to think so little of himself to need to have this word as a staple in his vocabulary, even when he's referencing a white man? Now ask yourself, what do we need to do as a culture and a society to begin to change this behavior?

I personally have never used the word, even privately or among my black friends. The reason is that what you do in private ultimately comes out in public, especially these days, with the proliferation of social media. As a recent case proves—one can be sitting in the privacy of one's own phone and inadvertently press a button on your phone—and voila, your entire conversation is broadcast live over Facebook.

This problem is particularly stark among an older generation of whites who see their power and status challenged by an increasingly diverse, increasingly gender-balanced power structure in America. And it often comes across in very blunt terms. A recent episode was when a white retired couple was sitting on their couch watching the news and discussing the recent events surrounding Black Lives Matter.

Unbeknownst to them, one of their phones was broadcasting the conversation over Facebook Live. "I've got the emails about how we're supporting, and we need to fix this problem, f---you," said retired navy captain and US Naval Academy Alumni Association board member Scott Bethmann. He objected to the fact that organizations felt a necessity to publicly align themselves with Black Lives Matter—even when they themselves had done nothing wrong. "So, all the white people have to say something nice to the black bitch that works in the office." At one point during the rant, "Mr. Bethmann asks his wife if she is 'against the niggers?' after she complains about ethnic diversity."

The blowback was understandably harsh. Mr. Bethmann, a distinguished navy veteran, officer, and Naval Academy graduate, was forced to leave his distinguished seat on the Academy's alumni board and also had his membership in a private club in Jacksonville, Florida, where he resides, revoked. This was undoubtedly a high price to pay for such a brief moment of indiscretion. It may have permanently sullied a lifetime of otherwise good deeds and exceptional service to our country.

The lesson here is simple but germane to the topic at hand. What you practice in private ultimately becomes public. As noted author and businessman Steven Covey once wrote in his excellent book, *Spiritual Roots of Human Relations*, "We do not have a successful public victory—that is, an accomplished worthy task—unless we have a successful private victory." That is, what we produce in public comes from how we prepare our minds and hearts in private.

What is in a man's heart will eventually come out of his mouth. A recent and alarming case of several police officers in Wilmington, North Carolina, illustrates the point even further. Officer Michael "Kevin" Piner told another officer he predicted Black Lives Matter protests would soon lead to civil war. "I am ready," Piner said. "We are just going to go out and start slaughtering them fucking niggers." The conversation continued on for over an hour and also involved a third officer, with repeated use of the N-word and numerous espousals of violence against African Americans. The officers' vile conversation came to light purely by chance. According to the *Washington Post*, "A sergeant was conducting routine video reviews when she found a nearly two-hour-long clip from Piner's cruiser created by an accidental activation."[2]

The officers were ultimately fired by the Wilmington police chief, who happens to be black. Furthermore, more than ninety of their previous arrest cases are under review, and several convictions based on their testimony have either been dropped or thrown out before adjudication.

These officers, who were senior officers with decades of experience, will likely never serve in a law enforcement capacity again. Nor should they. They failed privately—in what they thought was a private conversation—which caused them to fail publicly.

It becomes part of our character and seeps out at times we least expect it. The best course of action is to avoid using this sort of language altogether. In the N-word case, using such derisive and disrespectful terms belies a profound disrespect to anyone you're conversing with—no matter the race of the listener or speaker. It is highly advisable to eliminate that word from your vocabulary altogether.

---

2   Elfrink, Tim. "'We are just gonna go out and start slaughtering them': Three cops fired after racist talk of killing black residents." *Washington Post*, June 25, 2020, https://www.washingtonpost.com/nation/2020/06/25/wilmington-racist-police-recording/.

D. "Am I Even Allowed to Say That?"—How White Racial Anxiety Stymies Dialogue

Once we get past the obvious faux pas that the guardrails of prudence and integrity between our public and private personas help us to avoid, we are still in a sense stuck with a dilemma in terms of how to actually engage with the question of race. It is perhaps one of the great ironies of race that people who feel they have the most at stake in terms of having an open dialogue are too often afraid to begin one for fear of backlash or retaliation. This has created a real, tangible feeling of anxiety in many whites.

This is where we also begin to see white guilt. Many whites desire to help but fall prey to their own need for significance and end up fueling the very anger that is now consuming our nation. These white individuals in most cases are not truly taking the time to dig into the real issues or walk that country mile in the shoes of the race they are standing for; they are just acting out, and in this display, they are finding temporary bereavement from their pain, only to grant that pain more power over them in the long run.

In his article titled "Being White in Philly," Robert Huber laments the feeling of anxiety he encountered when his son, a freshman at Tulane, moved to an off-campus apartment in a crime-ridden neighborhood in Philadelphia near Tulane's campus.[3] He felt concerned for his son's safety in the majority-black neighborhood but was also afraid to bring up his concerns with fellow white colleagues and administrators at the university.

What they saw as a "gentrification" story—imagining condominiums and coffee shops springing up amidst the urban decay—he saw as a minefield of racial antagonism bubbling

---

3   Hubert, Robert. "Being White in Philly." *Philadelphia*, March 1, 2013, https://www.phillymag.com/news/2013/03/01/white-philly/.

just beneath the surface. He was loath to give voice to his concerns because he feared that retribution. "The problems," Huber writes, "seem intractable. In so many quarters, simply discussing race is seen as racist. Thus, white people are stuck, dishonest by default, as we take a pass on the state of this city's largely black inner city and settle for politely opening doors at Wawa before we slip back to our own lives."

Huber raises a poignant point: that a desire to avoid conflict results in whites portraying a feigned politeness around blacks that comes off as phony and dishonest. This dishonesty, which is implicitly felt by blacks, adds to the mistrust and creates an unspoken resentment that can often spill over into conflicts, resulting in further mistrust and misunderstanding. The stories that we all have seen and been told from both black and whites over time have burned fear into the hearts of young individuals who are seeking unity yet are unsure how to coexist in environments where the white boy sees a black boy wearing a doo-rag and his pants around his knees calling him the N-word every ten seconds; the black boy is feeling this prototypically privileged white boy sizing him up as the stereotyped thug, and therefore the division continues.

Here is the crux of the dilemma of race. We each experience anxiety and judgment, but what we all crave are understanding and significance. We must ask whether facing the fear and attempting to cross the chasm, risking revealing our own insecurities, is worth the ultimate result of unification.

However, there is also another dilemma: our loss of connection and community. It takes a practiced blindness to walk around in a gentrifying community and enter the coffee shops and bars and boutiques, yet ignore the obviously dire plight of those long-term residents who can only peer in—but never quite participate. But the ever-insightful Huber rightly observes that the sense of anomie and dislocation affects not only the poor black residents but also the whites.

"We're stuck in another way, too," he says. "Our troubled black communities create in us a tangle of feelings, including this one: a desire for things to be better. But for that sentiment to come true—for it to mean anything, even—I've come to believe that white people have to risk being much more open. It is impossible to know how that might change the racial dynamics in Philadelphia or the plight of the inner city. But as things stand, our cautiousness and fear mean that nothing changes in how blacks and whites relate, and most of us lose out on the possibility of what Jen has found: real connection."

In search of real connection, we have allowed ourselves to be emotionally vulnerable. Anyone who has built a deep connection with another person—whether a child or a spouse or a close friend—has, at times, revealed things about themselves they are not comfortable revealing to anyone. Whether intentionally or unconsciously, we let our guards down among people we love and trust. In fact, we may even believe that we have let our guard down because we love and trust the other person. But the process actually occurs in the reverse sequence. By letting our guard down, we in fact catalyze the process of building love and trust with another person. Guard down first. Love and trust next.

I have a successful white colleague who works on the ground level and invests millions of dollars into impoverished black communities, and he actually agrees with the fact that he and his staff must open up and let their guard down before they can really make a difference in these neighborhoods. This takes commitment to the process and elimination of our own programming to reach the masses. The story is so thick and runs so deep that it takes time to turn around, but they have found a way to do it, and it is done through experiencing and understanding, then working together for the empowerment of all involved.

Are there risks inherent in this process of trust-building? Of course there are. Someone to whom you reveal something personal about yourself could actually turn around and use it against you. They could manipulate you. They could reveal your secrets to strangers. They could judge or hate you. But what if they don't? What if showing your human frailty touches their own sense of vulnerability and begins to create a bond? This can and does happen, as well.

The decision to let someone in comes down to this: what are the stakes? Does the value of making the possible connection outweigh the risks of rejection? This is something that we, as human beings, irrespective of race, gender, culture, religion, or sexual orientation, struggle with constantly. Nevertheless, it is the fundamental question we all have to ask of ourselves if we truly wish to resolve the dilemma of race in this country. What is at stake? Is the risk worth the reward? I think if you dig deep enough, if you are committed enough, you will discover the answer; the truth for you always lies within.

E. Gradually Build Dialogue through Consistent and Rigorous Practice

We know instinctively that doing nothing in the face of the social upheaval we are experiencing will not work. There is too much at stake, for our country and for the world. We also know that reacting negatively will not further the process of social connection we are seeking. Furthermore, merely avoiding tough conversations and "virtue signaling" our way of out this dilemma won't work either. It just compounds the dishonesty and makes the situation worse. Alas, the only way forward is, well . . . forward. And that is going to require some degree of confrontation. The question is, how do we frame the engagement, and what are the rules? Are we going to blindly and foolishly follow the crowds, or are we going to be freethinkers that seek and experience the right way to move forward, the right way as individuals and as a country?

The first thing not to do is to nominate the first black person you see as the honorary referee of the race Olympics. No, black folks are just as exhausted as you are, perhaps even more so because they have no room for retreat into a totally accepting culture into which they can blend seamlessly. There is going to have to be dialogue, but it will first start with an inner dialogue among whites to determine, in a safe space, what their concerns and hang-ups are. I say an inner dialogue among whites because the degree of familiarity in terms of kinship and culture creates an easier rapport and a more forgiving environment. No one is going to have to "virtue signal" or "parrot act" just to prove they are not racist in front of their black friends or colleagues, or worse yet, to themselves.

However, after that, after some of the rough edges have been worked out, we all need to get in rooms together, across the country—whether at the office, the gym, the church, the restaurant, or the bar—and begin to have a dialogue. It will initially seem quite awkward, quite fraught, but as Kwame Christian, director of the American Negotiation Institute, says, "The best things in life are on the other side of difficult conversations."

Christian outlines a framework for dialogue in which individuals can use "compassionate curiosity to find confidence in conflict." Negotiation is the art of turning win-lose or lose-lose into win-win.

1. Seek to Understand First
The first step in the process is to seek to understand before being understood. In fact, if this were the only step, and each side

applied it, we would probably need very little further discussion. But in seeking to understand, you are assuming your own ignorance as to the other person's motives and reasons.

You are truly curious about where they're coming from. And by exhibiting this curiosity, you are showing them that although you may not agree with them completely, you respect their humanity, intellect, and life experiences, and you are willing to get to ground level and walk an entire day or even a week in their shoes. Having seemingly opposing sides work together for the greater good of a community (so they can see that they both want the same thing) is the most significant way to break down the walls and build lasting trust. The military has done this for years, and I have seen blacks and whites lay down their lives to rescue their brothers because of this beautiful bond.

2. Value Authenticity over Elegance

Many times, our communications with others get lost in translation. Even when the two (or more) speak fluent English amongst each other, words and their meanings get filtered through the lens of our personal experiences, biases, fears, and cultural conditioning. Things that are meant one way are bound to sound a different way to a listener coming from another perspective. We relish in and hold on to identifying with our story, rarely with any consideration for the stories of others.

Assuming that the person you are engaging with means well—and that either they or, in many cases, you yourself may be misinformed—can allow a new way of seeing them. As long as they are stating their honest opinion, we have to accept it. After all, the only test here is commitment to honesty, not determining objective truth. We must understand that we all have A Truth and that we must accept A Truth's relativity until we have experienced it firsthand, and even then, there may be differences we have to accept. We must also be humble in the understanding that there is only One Absolute Truth, and we will not know nor understand that until we stand before God.

The Bible says, "A man's wisdom gives him patience; it is to his glory to overlook an offense" (Proverbs 19:11, NIV). If we are going to begin to open up to each other and be vulnerable, we have to have patience. Taking offense where none is intended (we are assuming good intent, remember) is a clear sign that we are impatient.

VII. The Path Forward: A Twelve-Step Approach

A. Preface: The Widening Gyre

In the recent chaotic swirl following the public execution of Mr. George Floyd, the foundational underpinnings of the American culture are under siege. Nonminority Americans are newly confronted with the centuries-old issue of race. A path forward toward broader understanding, deeper interracial relationships, and the expansion of liberty to include all Americans is proposed.

B. Step One: Listen

> *"My dear brothers and sisters, take note of this: Everyone should be quick to listen, slow to speak and slow to become angry." (James 1:19)*

As a child we're taught the importance of listening by our parents and elders. We've all been told that you have to listen first before you act, but we are also told you must listen in order to learn. What is the importance of listening that we must all ask ourselves? Listen innocently, actively, and to everyone you can. Listen to the tales of young men with hostile police encounters, athletes, neighbors. Take it all in. The anger, pent up as it has been for decades. Like a traveler recounting his experience after returning from a remote land, pay attention to the details. The intensity, rage, and anguish. "Him who knows the country gives direction to him who asks the way," we read in the Ninth Mandala of the *Rigveda*. This jostling experience of police hostility is not broadly known outside the minority communities and is as if the tale of an unfamiliar land.

However, that is perhaps a part of the disconnect between blacks and whites, that there isn't a shared understanding from whites of the plight of their fellow Americans, and when you don't understand that which you've never experienced, it becomes incredibly difficult to empathize with the plight and experience of those who are outwardly different.

C. Step Two: A Common Purpose

"Can two walk together, except they be agreed?" (Amos 3:3)

As we settle down into listening, what was initially foreign and unknown experience becomes more intimate, shared, and fully understood. Amos famously writes that two men walking together need to share a common purpose. Nonminority Americans need now to be still, raptly listen, and cultivate a common experience. However, we must imagine how we ourselves would feel in a like situation regardless of the scenario to truly imagine what those who are different than us are experiencing. It is through this process that we can truly understand, and through understanding we can create change.

D. Step Three: The Divinity of All Creation

"God created mankind in his image, in the image of God he created them, male and female he made them." (Genesis 1:28)

In settling into listening and establishing rapport, the shared ground basis of identity of all human life becomes progressively evident. What we have in common far and away exceeds our differences. It is easy to be in contempt of what we don't ourselves know. Empathy grows with familiarity, and familiarity is what brings people together and fosters unity.

E. Step Four: Bear No Shame

"The son shall not suffer for the iniquity of the father."
(Ezekiel 18:20)

Building relationships cannot be self-effacing. We don't invite our friend to dinner and ourselves vacate the table. We share the same space and take the same meal. In extending ourselves as nonminority Americans to our minority brethren, we don't abandon our own traditions or shame ourselves or our Nation. We cannot confess to sins we did not ourselves commit. Free and sovereign people solve their own problems and it is now our endeavor to expand the mantle of full-throated Liberty to all.

F. Step Five: Maintain Hope

"For I know the plan I have for you," declares the Lord, "plans
to prosper you and not to harm you, plans to give you hope and
a future." (Jeremiah 29:11)

A new nihilism has risen up in the current moment. It is held that no matter what we do, the yoke of racism is built into our history and identity. Oppression, bigotry, and injustice arise inevitably from our founding and like Original Sin are an inescapable element of life in America. History speaks powerfully to the contrary. Progress has been made. We are no longer mired in the antebellum South or the oppression of Jim Crow. Fifty years of earnest efforts at racial reconciliation have been of great benefit to the African American community. Liberty is the American elixir and yet further expanding Liberty is the mission at hand.

G. Step Six: Be Courageous

> *"David also said to Solomon his son,*
> *'Be strong and courageous and do the work. Do not be afraid or*
> *discouraged. . .'" (1 Chronicles 15:58)*

In the fire-breathing rhetoric of the moment there is a new tyranny arising. It unabashedly shames and bullies. Deviation of thought is not tolerated, and consensus must be complete and immediate. It is akin to a new Stalinism with toppling statues and renamed boulevards. We need to remind ourselves that Liberty has been the greatest engine of productivity in human history, having lifted countless billions out of poverty, and remains the cornerstone of our American identity. The times demand that as we listen, deepen empathy, and more fully experience our shared identity, we at the same time remain steadfast advocates for freedom and the rule of law. Centuries ago Paul instructed Corinthians to "stand firm. Let nothing move you." (1 Corinthians 15:58)

H. Step Seven: Prosperity

> *"You shall remember the Lord your God, for it is he who gives*
> *you power to get wealth, that he may confirm his covenant that*
> *he swore to your fathers, as it is this day." (Deuteronomy 8:18)*

At the center of African American culture is a conservative core that emphasizes family, faith, and industry. Equal opportunity initiatives were instituted in the 1960s. Over the ten years from 1961 to 1971, Caucasian family income in America rose by 31 percent, while African American income rose by 55 percent. Among individuals of college age, the percentage who actually enrolled in college remained unchanged between 1965 and 1972 among whites but nearly doubled among African Americans.

Likewise, the number of professionals among whites increased by about one fifth between 1965 and 1972. It nearly doubled among African American families. The number of black engineers tripled. Simply removing barriers to entry appeared to be all that was necessary to unleash the skills, talents, and endeavor embedded within the black community. The expansion of Liberty resulting from the removal of barriers to entry prompted this flourishing prosperity. Large government programs were also initiated at this time, though their impact is difficult to assess. Rising minimum wages made entry level work harder to find, and large welfare programs made work less essential. Policies of affirmative action have not had discernible impact on the African American community beyond what was achieved with the expansion of opportunity.[4]

President John F. Kennedy famously pointed out that all boats rise with the tide. This experience of now over fifty years ago bears this out. It is particularly instructive to consider this experience in the current era when the issue of income inequality is raised. The individual, unleashed and unfettered, creates wealth. We read in the Scripture that when life is lived within God's Law, "then you will make your way prosperous, and then you will have good success" (Joshua 1:8).

I. Step Eight: Build Endurance

"And let steadfastness have its full effect, that you may be perfect and complete, lacking in nothing." (James 1:4)

---

4 Sowell, Thomas. *Ethnic America: A History* (New York: Basic Books, 1981), p. 223.

Coming together, breaking rank, and leaving tribal packs is a risky proposition. As white Americans begin to listen to their black brethren, cultivate relationships, have a deepening effect on one another, and allow the Venn diagrams of our lives to more completely overlap, there will be resistance. The faster the arrow flies, the greater the resistance it encounters. As we stray a little further from our usual boundaries, the tether of habit, custom, and tradition will pull back with greater resistance. Look at what is on your bookshelf. Read something new. Consider who you have fun with on the golf or tennis court. Reach out to someone new. Consider your place of worship. Good chance they worship the same God at a Church down the road. The oxygen that feeds the fire of the rage and enmity now engulfing our nation is our separateness, divisions, acrimony, and tribalism.

These are the most treacherous times in generations. The temptation will be to fall back to our centers. Resist the urge. Open the aperture. Endure in the campaign and snuff out the fire. Paul appealed to the Corinthians, exhorting that "there be no divisions among you, but that you be united in the same mind and the same judgment" (1 Corinthians 1:10-13).

J. Step Nine: Have Fun

"A glad heart makes a cheerful face, but by sorrow of heart the spirit is crushed." (Proverbs 15:13)

These tasks now incumbent upon white Americans are not arduous and joyless. In fact, they depend for their success on expanding our pleasure. Sigmund Freud emphasized the Pleasure Principle in relationships. We are attracted to sources of pleasure and fulfillment and seek them out. Affection will deepen with familiarity. Rooting for the same team and fishing for the same bass are plain good fun. In doing that we are building something new. As the great Irish poet William Butler Yeats wrote: "All things fall and are built again, and those that build them are gay."

K. Step Ten: Humility

"With all humility and gentleness, with patience, bearing one another in love . . ." (Ephesians 4:2)

The four centuries of the American experience have resulted in the greatest enduring civilization in history. From the time of the ratification of the Constitution to the first quarter of the twentieth century, mankind advanced more than had been the case in the 10,000 years that preceded the founding of the new nation. In 1789, one went to sleep in rooms lit by tapered candles. In 1916, electric lights were everywhere. Vaccines had been developed, Halsted performed surgery for breast cancer, goods were transported across the continent by rail, and the steam engine propelled ships and locomotives. Countless millions were lifted from abject poverty into a burgeoning middle class through the engine of capitalism supported by personal sovereignty and limited government. Yet no single group authored this great leap forward. This was a collaborative achievement. It represented hybrid vigor. Some 45,000,000 human beings from all over the world immigrated to America and together were the inventors of this dazzling new City on the Hill. Once here, they reinvented themselves while cobbling together this new Nation. Chow mein was developed by the Chinese in America. There is no Afro hairdo in Africa.

Freedom, then, invented America. No single race or group can lay claim to it. We are all its proud parents. "But the one who looks into the perfect law, the law of liberty, and perseveres, being no hearer who forgets but a doer who acts, he will be blessed in his doing" (James 1:25).

L. Step Eleven: Lawfulness

"Let every person be subject to the governing authorities . . .
Therefore whoever resists the authorities resists what God has
appointed, and those who resist will incur judgment." (Romans
13: 1-7)

From its founding, the American nation has asserted equal protection under the law. The second sentence of the Declaration of
Independence asserts: "We hold these truths to be self-evident,
that all men are created equal." The Fourteenth Amendment of
the Constitution was later ratified in 1868 and decrees that "no
state shall . . . deny to any person within its jurisdiction the equal
protection of the laws." White Americans need to ask themselves
if this is currently the case. Sentencing disparity has been a viti-
ating element for broad swaths of our population and a source
of enragement and disenfranchisement particularly among
minority communities. Lengthy sentences for drug violations
have, it is asserted, routinely been meted out to citizens of color,
while much lighter sentences for the same or similar crimes are
received by white offenders. The black/white sentencing disparity has reportedly been increasing over the recent years and has
been a root cause of the recent social unrest.

The potential causes for this widely reported inequality are
many, ranging from residing in higher-crime neighborhoods
leading to increased police contacts and establishment of a prior
record to inherent raw racial bias in both prosecutorial discre-
tion and judges' imposition of sentences.

Law-abiding Caucasians may well be thoroughly unac-
quainted with these issues and have an entirely different collective experience with the legal system. Listening to African
Americans, deepening rapport and growth of shared experience
will oblige them to now review these issues and take the scale
firmly in hand. James Baldwin wrote that "Not everything that

is faced can be changed. But nothing can be changed until it is faced."

Disparity in dispensation of justice is itself a kind lawlessness. While we are all now painfully aware of the lawlessness of marauding crowds robbing and vandalizing in recent weeks, this perception of unequal protection under the law quietly dates back decades. It is incumbent on us all, even amidst injustice, to conduct ourselves lawfully. After centuries of having his people brutally enslaved, the burning bush instructed that Moses petition the Pharaoh for freedom for his people. God had heard the groaning of his people and He led them to freedom. Paul wrote: "Let every person be subject to the governing authorities" (Romans 13:1). This while he himself was imprisoned and awaiting execution. We can't ourselves abandon the law while simultaneously pursuing justice.

M. Step Twelve: Beginning Anew

"Remember not the former things, nor consider the things of old. Behold, I am doing a new thing; now it springs forth, do you perceive it?" (Isaiah 43:18-19)

Guilt, accusation, and the weight of the past are an encumbrance in navigating a path forward. White Americans imbued with an understanding of and deepening affection for African Americans are far better partners in doing what free people do, which is to solve their own problems. White Americans need now to listen to their African American brethren, grow in affection and intention, believe that they can together formulate solutions, be true to their own traditions while extending themselves to others, endure in the effort, and assert the sovereignty of law while simultaneously pursuing greater justice.

The founders of the twelve-step program, Mr. Bill Wilson and Dr. Robert Holbrook Smith, sat in a living room in Akron,

Ohio, in 1935 and crafted the most successful approach to addiction management of all time. Squarely facing the addiction, confessing the need for God's support, examining the past, and learning to live a new life was the formula for finding the path forward. The twelfth step of Mr. Wilson and Dr. Smith's program called for the spiritually renewed and recovering addict to commit to sharing this new understanding with others ensnared by addiction. So it is now as we apply these steps to move toward racial reconciliation. The change in sensibilities accrued through this twelve-step program need to be shared with other white Americans as we together move from the fatigue and listlessness of our past toward the exhilaration and power of our future. This moment requires that we all not so much see ourselves as we have been or even as we are, but instead imagine what we together could be.

VIII. Achieve Economic Emancipation

In April 2019, I had the pleasure of being invited by Washington, DC's mayor, Muriel Bowser, to speak at a breakfast gathering honoring DC Emancipation Day, where we celebrated the 157th anniversary of Lincoln's formal emancipation of over 3,000 enslaved individuals in the District, on April 16, 1862. Several months later President Lincoln would go on to issue the Emancipation Proclamation, on January 1, 1863, which legally emancipated the nation's estimated millions of slaves. In this year's commemoration, the District's political leadership and distinguished citizens pushed for what they consider to be a last frontier in the quest for emancipation—the establishment of statehood for the District.

It almost boggles my mind that a year later, protesters are demanding the statue honoring Lincoln's (and our nation's) noble sacrifice to free our ancestors be torn down. Why? Will they demand the hundreds of thousands of African Americans named 'Lincoln' change their names? Will they next demand that Lincoln University, an HBCU named for the great emancipator, repudiate its namesake? A year ago, this would have seemed patently absurd. Now it's distinctly in the realm of possibility.

Our history certainly isn't one that is perfect, no history is, but demanding the removal of President Lincoln is a bridge too far. Are George Washington and Thomas Jefferson next? Again, none of these men were perfect, but they left behind a system that would permit us to expand and grow into better angels and that should not and must not be ignored. What we have inherited must be analyzed and assessed. We throw away that which is bad, and we preserve and protect that which is good, including our imperfect leaders. After all, if it were not for Lincoln's courageous act, what would have become of the slaves? It goes without saying that nature at some point would run its course and they would become free, but when? How long would they have remained enslaved? Perhaps the South would have remained its own country where blacks continued under such a terrifying system. These things must not ever be overlooked, but it seems far too many people, particularly our young people, are completely missing that point.

But back to April 2019. I was somewhat surprised to be invited to the event because I am not a supporter of statehood for the District. I believe the founders of our nation had wise and practical reasons for leaving the district out of the American federation of states. They rightly reasoned that including the District within any state's boundaries—as had been originally done—would reduce the District's role as neutral ground where state representatives could come together to hash out the nation's business. This was necessary for the District's laws and taxes to affect representatives of the other states, thereby creating political pressure on one state to do another state's bidding. I believe the soundness of this decision has stood the test of time.

However, that does not mean that many of the District's residents have yet to experience full "emancipation." I do not mean emancipation in the political and legal sense, but emancipation in the form of economic independence. You can never truly be free until you have the means to dictate your own path and design the future for yourself, your family, and your community, and you can only do that through economic means. You can only do that if you have the ability to orchestrate your one destiny, and in order to do that, you must have financial freedom. Otherwise, you become beholden to others who will dictate your every move. That's not freedom—in fact that's a form of slavery itself, not in the brutal sense, but economic dependence means you're beholden to others and your life is centered around that as a means of existence.

As I prepared my remarks for the breakfast, I realized that I might be marching into somewhat hostile territory, as most in attendance were supporters of statehood. However, I did feel that I had something important to contribute to the discussion of emancipation and what it truly means. I thought back to my own family, and how my earliest known ancestor, my great-great-grandfather Luke Howard, had been born a slave on a plantation in Marion County, South Carolina, in 1805. During his lifetime he witnessed not only the height of the cotton aristocracy in the American South, but also Lincoln's election, the founding of the Republican Party, the Civil War, and the emancipation of all the slaves.

In the aftermath of the Civil War, most of my slave ancestors stayed on at the plantations where they had been formerly enslaved. Some, who fought as Union soldiers in the Civil War believed that Lincoln, the Great Emancipator, would award them land taken from the plantations of their former owners.

This was not to transpire. Several black Civil War veterans wrote to General Howard (after whom DC's famed historically black university is named) to complain that the federal government in Washington had betrayed them.

One of them wrote to General Howard in 1867:

> If the government having concluded to befriend Its late enemies and to neglect to observe the principles of common faith between Itself and us Its allies In the war you said was over, now takes away from them all right to the soil they stand upon save such as they can get by again working for your late and their all-time enemies. If the government does so we are left in a more unpleasant condition than our former . . . [condition of slavery].

In other words, the returning veterans knew that without the ability to build an economic foundation, the emancipated would be reduced to a condition that was in many ways worse than their former condition. The federal government did not respond to their requests and essentially abandoned them. Then-President Andrew Jackson, who wanted to heal the deep wounds of the war, restored the lands to their original owners, the very people against whom the federal government had just waged a bitter internecine war.

This was a painstakingly slow progress that would take several generations to produce fruit. There was very little in the way of redemption. Shortly after the war, the Klu Klux Klan and other white vigilante groups began terrorizing the former slaves. Laws were passed, including the Jim Crow laws, that denied blacks the basic rights of citizenship—they were restricted from voting, participating on juries, and even bringing lawsuits in state courts. When you have stolen from someone, it is not enough to merely stop the theft. Justice requires that you redeem the value of what was taken. In many cases this was not done, and the lasting effects of slavery and de jure segregation continue to this day in the form of entrenched poverty and social stigma.

The former slaves found themselves nominally "free," abandoned by the government, but practically still enslaved. They did own, at least nominally, the fruits of their own labor, though. And so, they started from nothing, working harder than they had ever worked to establish some form of economic foundation. Not only did they continue to toil in the fields of their former enslavers—albeit now for wages—but many even developed sharecroppers and other forms of land-lease arrangements, where they did extra work to secure their own land and capital.

This legacy lasted up until my own generation. My father was eventually able to save up enough money from laboring and sharecropping to purchase his own farm, which eventually became self-sufficient and produced wealth for our family. However, it took almost five generations from when Lincoln formally emancipated the slaves until my family finally discovered true freedom. This demonstrates that curating true economic freedom is a process that is seldom sought in the lifetime of one generation but is a process that normally occurs across several.

The painstaking work it took over successive generations to bring forth a viable black middle class should not be taken for granted. It is not enough to merely be proclaimed "emancipated" without also providing some method of redress. That is why, in the absence of some sort of redemption, it is very difficult, if not impossible, to achieve true freedom.

But true freedom comes at a price. In the words of seventeenth-century Irish statesman John Philpot Curran, "The condition upon which God hath given liberty to man is eternal vigilance; which condition if he break, servitude is at once the consequence of his crime and the punishment of his guilt." The American colonists, most notably Patrick Henry, would take up this rallying cry in their fight against British tyranny. *Vigilance* is an interesting word. It is more than mere observation or awareness. It is indeed a commitment to remaining observant and aware.

The best predictor of success when it comes to economic emancipation is to be committed to the task. Free enterprise has been the greatest engine of wealth ever devised in human history. It has raised countless billions from abject poverty over the centuries and that continues to be the case today. The wealthiest man in history, Mr. John D. Rockefeller, had four pillars of prosperity:

1. Big problems require bold action
2. We need to use all the tools in our belt to solve big problems
3. Profit and social impact are not mutually exclusive
4. Families can play a leading role

These axioms are as universally applicable now as they were in the nineteenth century but require a relentless commitment to the task at hand. The perception that pursuit of success represents cultural betrayal creates a dual-mindedness that undermines success. Among African Americans, the hazard of "acting white" has been attached to the pursuit of good grades, personal achievement, and accrual of wealth. The sense that one's blackness is diminished by academic success, skill set development, and unfettered ambition is tremendously demoralizing, particularly for young African Americans. We don't think about the fact that when you look at African American opportunities and success stories today, they were nonexistent at this level and magnitude just sixty years ago. We don't stop to think about the progress because some have become so stuck and focused on the past that it is all they know. It consumes them so much that thinking about the present to build for the future is a foreign idea, but it is an idea that has caused great stagnation, and in some arenas, it has caused drastic decline. Certainly, those of the past wouldn't be happy with that mindset; they would move forward and not allow the history of the past to stall progress of the future. They would demand that we all be committed to continuing to become better by challenging ourselves to rise to the highest levels. They would say to continue to push and continue to demand the best out of each other. I'm certain of this because it is what my family taught me and my siblings. Their accomplishments weren't enough—they wanted us to continue to move forward and we did, setting new goals and accomplishing new things for the next generation to pick up the mantle as we did from our parents.

Mr. Rockefeller held that personal success and social impact are not mutually exclusive. The only self-made billionaire African American woman is Ms. Oprah Winfrey, who is the embodiment of Rockefeller's third principle. She has amassed an enormous personal fortune in media, is a household name across the country, and yet has developed that success while raising issues of racial equality and gender equity. She has not retreated from her identity as an African American or as a woman and has enjoyed the support and viewership of all races and genders in contemporary America. Like Rockefeller, she has used her notoriety and financial success to richly contribute to the general welfare through support of education, advocacy for girls and women's issues, and deepening spiritual awareness. In 1989, when she was inducted into the Academy of Achievement, she pointed out: "It doesn't matter who you are, where you come from. The ability to triumph begins with you. Always."

Embracing the possibility of success, being unapologetic about pursuit of early academic achievement, establishing personal expertise, and crafting success from that platform is the sine qua non (without which there is none) of winning. These prerequisites need to be lustily pursued. The crippling burden of deep ambivalence about winning or half-hearted undertaking of achievement need to be disavowed in the African American community. They are the quicksand of personal and cultural victory. On July 16, 2009, President Obama rightly pointed out that "No one has written your destiny for you. Your destiny is in your hands . . . That's what we have to teach all our children. No excuses."

We depart from this understanding at our own peril. By accepting the premise that obstacles are too great to overcome, that disadvantages of family or circumstance are overwhelming, we invite the Devil into the room. If there is no real prospect for a fulfilling future, then we are left with just the legacy of the past and the poverty of the moment. That is not to say that the past isn't important or that we should remember it as a reminder of where we once were, but you have to be forward thinking if you seek to not stay stagnant. There is no future to build, no greatness to embrace, and no dream to chase. Why learn languages, decline verbs, and solve algebraic equations when in fact there is no path forward?

Like crossing the River Lethe in Dante's *Inferno*, there hangs the sign: "Abandon Hope, All Ye Who Enter Here." It is a cruel hoax to advance the notion of hopelessness, despair, and the inevitability of all dreams to be crushed and all aspirations unfulfilled. The vision of the future animates the ambitions of the present. We need them both.

Although I've written extensively in the past on the subject of money, there are always new facets that come to my mind as time goes on. One of the most important things in terms of African American advancement is the critical role of wealth in family relationships. The ability to contribute financially to one's family and to be a source of support in times of need is one of the most important and beneficial uses of wealth.

My latest musings on the subject came about in a very interesting way. I was recently speaking to a friend whose son had not long ago been admitted to a top private school. He has always been an exemplary father, attending his son's sports activities, disciplining his son, and instilling confidence in his child's young spirit. In a word, he's been there for his son through thick and thin. And as a result, his son has grown up to be quite an impressive young man: a straight-A student, champion athlete, and a leader among his peers.

But my friend has always struggled financially. And when the opportunity for his child to attend a private school arose, he finds it quite distressing to come up with a means to pay the tuition. As a friend I want to help him, but I'm not so sure exactly how to do so. I could marshal support among my peers and raise a scholarship fund. And perhaps that would help in the short term. But I can't help feeling that at the end of the day one of the things a father should bestow upon a son is a sense of ability to be a provider. I'm not knocking families in which the mother is a breadwinner, that is certainly a perfectly fine arrangement, but the core essence of manhood is an ability to provide materially for one's family. These are the traditional values I was raised with, along with, of course, treating one's fellow human beings with compassion and justice and being humble before one's creator. I use the example of my friend not to ask for sympathy or pity, but to showcase how not having financial freedom can limit not just your own dreams, but the dreams of your child, which has generational impact.

There is a certain amount of pride in being able to support one's family. It tends to elevate the individual within the family order and create respect and admiration. I find in my own family that the ability to provide avenues for opportunity and communion—whether helping a sibling with a business venture or paying for travel and hosting family gatherings—has brought our large family much closer together. Furthermore, members of the family tend to admire those who have done well financially and aspire to become like them. In that way, achieving financial success has a great impact upon family aspirations and achievement. It sets the precedent for others to expect to do well and similarly adopt the moral and ethical habits that attaining wealth often requires.

But it is not merely the effect of being able to directly contribute financially that enables the wealthy person to be a leader in one's family. There are also other things. The fact that wealth enables one to acquire better education, to take better care of one's health, and generally to build social relationships with other accomplished and successful people also becomes a family benefit. The ability to call up a business contact and open the doors of opportunity to a younger family member is one of the ways in which wealth is transferred to subsequent generations.

There are so many problems that can be solved by having money. You can get better medical care if you are sick, and employ people to help with tasks that are time-consuming and routine, thus freeing one's time up to focus on the really important things in life. It's also possible to travel and expand one's horizons, and to acquire possessions that make life more enjoyable. Life shouldn't just be all work without time and the ability to enjoy it. No man or woman should live just to work, because there is so much more to life and since each of us is only given one life, we must enjoy every aspect of it and should be able to do so unrestricted without worrying or feeling burdened by not having enough. Money enables us to take our children to new places to experience new cultures and different people. It enables the ability to have well-rounded and well-balanced children who can then excel academically and excel as adults in life.

Having money enables us to prepare our children to excel. Just as my father was able to pay for me and my siblings to get a college education and to have varying experiences, none of this would have been possible without financial resources. Just imagine the capabilities and the chances of grooming your kids to do well in life because you're able to unlock doors for them. Imagine not having to worry about being able to afford extracurricular activities, which builds up necessary life skills, but can also turn on the light bulb of ideas in creative and eager young people looking to explore and discover their place in the world. Being financially secure enables all of this; it opens the doors of opportunity in unparalleled ways, which is why it is so critical for more people to not only understand this concept, but to work as hard as they can to realize it. Having financial security isn't just about the now, it is also about the long term—it's about the future that is unseen that really signifies its importance.

So why, if having money has so many benefits, is the desire to become wealthy viewed with such scorn among some people in this country? There seems to be a growing sensibility among some that the wealthy are inherently greedy or selfish and don't care about their fellow human beings. Worse yet, some claim that people with money are working in cahoots to deny the opportunity to others. From my perspective this is a totally wrongheaded approach. It assumes that the blessing one person receives automatically diminishes the prospects for others. This is a scarcity mentality based upon fear and greed. This attitude is not just found among the poor, however. Some wealthy people also think this way.

However, it is a growing sentiment among all Americans of all races and age groups. A sense of being left behind and left out of the American dream. As most studies indicate that there is a growing wealth and income divide in America, so does hostility toward wealthy individuals increase, and unfortunately, it only appears to be getting worse. It's the old tale of the haves and the have-nots that may become America's greatest problem in the long run. I would be remiss if I didn't state that I'm extremely concerned about this and the long-term impact it will have on our great nation if we don't give it more attention. This is one sentiment that is unsustainable if not directly addressed. We have to ask ourselves why such a growing percentage of Americans is feeling cornered, why are so many feeling left out and left behind? Some have gone so far as to say that their American dream is gone. But that isn't the case, and we have to constantly remind people that the American dream is here for me and for you, as it is for them, if you are willing to put forth the work, time, and effort to actualize it.

We have to work better at encouraging all Americans to build sustainable wealth, but doing so will require significant discipline and a change in habit. It also means encouraging more inventorship and entrepreneurship; it means expanding opportunities to a greater portion of people. Now for our young people, it's a bit more complicated, in part because of the rising cost of student debt, which plagues the current generation unlike in the past. I remember when I went to college and my father was able to pay for me and those of my siblings who wanted to get an education. To be able to do that today is nearly impossible unless you are wealthy. This presents a significant problem for millions of Americans, particularly in our current climate, which dictates that a bachelor's degree isn't enough to be successful, one has to also have a master's degree—further compounding the debt problem and making it harder for today's young people to build wealth. Therefore, when you analyze this reality, it becomes easy to understand why so many Americans are turning against those they deem wealthy. It's not because they hate the rich, it's because they themselves feel as if they're never going to be able to obtain any wealth.

I believe God wants us to prosper, not just survive. He wants us to enjoy the bounties of the earth upon which we have been placed. If not, why would he have given us talents, desires, and ambitions? These are innate motivations within all of life to grow and live a better life. Every living organism seeks to maximize its chances for survival and propagation.

Money in this society is often a scorecard for how one has conducted one's life and signifies the impact one has had on the society at large. Having money demonstrates a concern for expanding one's own life and the lives of one's loved ones. Seen in this context, being rich is not only a right, but possibly also a duty.

African Americans, if taken as a national group, would have the world's sixth largest economy. If they put their money where their race is and step up to become owners instead of merely consumers and workers, they would advance very quickly in this country. America is a nation that highly values wealth and ownership. In fact, wealth and ownership are the keys to political influence and social transformation.

A well-placed focus on ownership would mark a departure from the usual stance that blacks have had toward dealing with racism, and would demonstrate the progress that this country has made toward obliterating racial discrimination. In the not so

distant past, even if some individual blacks had achieved financial wealth, their collective ability to use that wealth to achieve
social or political advancement might have been blocked for
other, non-economic reasons. The fact that the Trump administration and corporate America are inviting black entrepreneurs
to take a leadership role as business owners is a sign of maturity
on the part of society.

But it also marks an opportunity for African Americans to
mature as a group. Some American blacks have taken comfort in
a position of victimhood in this society. In some respects, it has
removed the responsibility to take control of their own lives. For
them, racism has been more of a crutch than an impediment, in
that it discounted personal failures and amplified personal success. The very fact that large-scale black ownership of significant
corporate assets remains a milestone despite the financial capacity of members of black community to build businesses is an
obvious example.

In potentially taking on the mantle of ownership, the issue
of character will remain front and center. Being black will not
make ownership any easier than for any other entrepreneur of
another race. It's one thing to play the victim and blame one's
circumstances on discrimination. It's another stance to take
responsibility for one's circumstances and succeed, not despite—
but in fact, because of the obstacles one faces and overcomes.
Ownership changes one's orientation toward life in that regard.

There is a unique opportunity for African Americans to create what has only been created a handful of times and to do so in
a way that yields lasting results. Think about Black Wall Street in
Tulsa, Oklahoma, and what the blacks there were able to accomplish. Today there are far more college-educated blacks, and the
net worth of the black community in its entirety far supersedes
what it was then, so it's very possible to recreate this. But blacks

will have to rise to the occasion, and I know they can because they've done it before and certainly can do it again.

One needs to merely study other cultures such as Africans who come to the United States and who are highly educated, even higher than whites. We can study other immigrant groups, such as Hispanics, who have done well in pockets of communities across the United States, having ownership within their communities to slowly spread wealth and real influence. And lastly, we can study the Jewish community, who like blacks have gone through centuries of trials and tribulations to become a successful community today. I point these groups out to showcase what is possible when groups work together toward a greater collective goal and how that objective can yield significant fruit that can be utilized and further expanded by generation after generation.

As a business owner, I rarely think about race or society or what's going on in someone else's mind or in their closet. The buck literally stops with me, and I find myself much more than fully engaged with the challenges of meeting payroll, generating new ideas, and providing quality products in the marketplace. There is a certain level of being above the fray that's necessary to manage such responsibilities. Employees may have the option of not showing up, but ownership is a 24/7 job with no days off. As an owner, one has a broader constituency than just the racial or social class to which one ascribes. In reality, owners themselves are owned by the marketplace. And because so much is riding on it—employees' families and careers, providing critical goods and services to society at large—ownership demands the very best from us.

The reality is that ownership of a business is not an entitlement that one assumes based on one's wealth, but is a job just like any other within an organization. It requires having the judgment to make certain sacrifices in furtherance of the overall success of the organization.

Ownership is the true goal of any person or group seeking true economic freedom. The road there doesn't come fast nor does it come easy, but it shouldn't deter groups and individuals from embarking upon the tough and challenging journey to accomplishing it. You can be free in one regard and still captive in another, and the problem for many in the African American community is that far too many people are still captive; they are captive to other people's dreams and ideas. Don't get me wrong, not everyone will be great leaders, not everyone will come up with transformative ideas that change a community, a nation, or maybe even the world. There will be a need for workers, but certainly more people could tap into their potential to release a flood of creativity.

The problem for some is that they don't realize what God has instilled in them. It's far too easy to excuse one's own plight than it is to look internally and labor through all of the shortcomings and excel in spite of the setbacks. That takes a serious level of accountability and perseverance that not all have shown a willingness to do. Therefore, the plight of many African Americans will remain a consistent theme in black communities across the United States until this changes. Race can't continue to be the de facto excuse because at some point we will truly reach a place where race is unimportant. When that occurs, what then will be the excuse, what then will be the systemic hindrance against progression?

At some point, the buck stops with the individual and you are only responsible for yourself. Yes, life is hard, yes, there will be challenges, but no one will give you anything and nor should they. You have to work hard, you have to be smart, you have to think both creatively and strategically. So then the challenge for blacks is to collectively move as a single unit to build as they have at various times in the past. There must be a recognition that many of the issues plaguing many in the black community aren't because of race, but because of the lack of economic access and opportunity. However, access and opportunity already exist within the black community if they would come together. Race wouldn't be so front and center if people knew they had economic freedom to do as they pleased; if they knew they could put their children through college; if they knew that they could earn great wages; if they knew that if they had a great idea, others in the community would buy into it and thus build titans of industry. African Americans will never feel or be free until this is accomplished and the quicker the vast majority realizes this, the quicker the community can move in a way that creates a new black community that truly realizes all that American has to offer.

IX. Don't Put God in a Box

We have become so sensitive as a society and so disassociated with who we are as individuals that we have decided to place ourselves in a box, and as of late, this is not just any box—this is a box with a divider. We have placed this divider in it to distort and separate ourselves from knowing our true Self or, worse yet, one another.

Our true identity is totally lost. Oh, and let us not stop at this box having a divider in it, also let's now separate it from the other boxes. And then let us give each box different privileges and see these boxes as separate from one another so that we can now make decisions as a global whole to show just how separate we are.

Each box is not only different, but is running against the other boxes in, oh, let's say a race. Now let's break this down into a human race, but do not stop there, why not just escalate this to human racism? There, now we have it, the perfect recipe for devising a country and making sure that we can never come together as one and actually demand a democracy that sees us as one and as a result acts as such.

Now you ask yourself, what these boxes are that Armstrong is speaking of? Well, these are the boxes that you check every time you fill out an application, every time you do business with the government, every time you register for a driver's license, every time you ask for government assistance, every time you get a loan for anything, every time you buy a gun, every time you sneeze, our government must place you in a box before you are issued that which you seek to purchase or get approval for.

Now you ask, what is this about a divided box? Well, why must blacks be cornered into being African Americans? Are we all from Africa? I know I'm not. I have a strong Cherokee heritage, and my father was not from Africa. We have black men from all over the globe that are Americans, and their ancestry and journey to America do not always identify with Africa for whatever reason. Then there are whites, and why not German whites or Russian whites? They are also Americans. There are many Native American tribes, yet you do not see Navajo Americans in the checkboxes.

Here is my point: it is time to eliminate all race, creed, or religion in the United States of America. We simply need to have a box that says American or Other. If you are a citizen of the United States, you simply check that box, end of story. We must start reeling our government in. I beg of you, my American citizens, stop supporting this nonsense. We must stop feeding our government's segregation of us as a country; we must stand up for life, liberty, and the pursuit of happiness for all Americans.

As I travel the world and throughout our country, I smile at the progress that we have made and the progress that we are living out in our everyday lives. I see a culture of every color under the sun living together in perfect harmony, cities running well and living in peace and everyone moving through this time and space with harmony.

Sure, you will have many bad things to exploit if that is what you choose to focus on, and that is your freedom, but get out of my way. You are free to wallow in your hell—let the rest of us move on, and continue to advance into a new world of love and compassion living as one nation united in one cause, a cause of Unity and Love.

We have given our government so much power, they have indeed taken us over so gradually that we have not even realized the water is boiling and we are in it. The government has become so bloated and overstaffed that it is harming our society. Every one of those individuals must prove their value and come up with something to regulate. This lets big government create more boxes to fit things into.

We have so-called health professionals, who live in boxes themselves and are forcing us to close our businesses, changing the guidelines for safety weekly while keeping six feet apart, just so they feel like they are in control. People, please wake up, we must take our power back, and I'm not talking black power or white power, I am talking American power. The power that our forefathers put into the Constitution of the United States, the power of a government for the people and by the people.

These so-called leaders of our government have been allowed to wield a double-edged sword that has kept us in a place of racism for far too long. I am not in any way saying that we need to take to the streets and run like wild animal mobs to try to get our point across. I'm saying that we must vote and vote consistently. We must take a stand that we don't elect officials that have not had any life experiences. We are electing leaders in this country every day who are straight out of college or out of college and in politics for a few years. These individuals have not lived a single day on the front lines. All they hear are stories, and without being on those front lines seeing and working through all the stories, then our country is being run on stories.

Our children *must* be encouraged to play and interact. Don't you see what is going on here, it starts with the boxes, then it moves to a bloated government to regulate the boxes. Then it's more stories and more regulations, fluffing everyone's pillow to get the votes. Then it's dictating our businesses and our children.

Socialism is next, and if you don't wake up to this, it will only be too late by the time the disaster is before us. We must take back our power; we must stop before we check a box and choose to do something different, draw a box beside the boxes that says American, and check that box. Then when they say you have to check a box, tell them you did, and if they insist, then say you would like to talk to their in-house lawyer about discrimination against you being an American. This is how we will make this shift. I implore you, America, stop the incessant flow of bias and agenda-driven media into your head, pause the TV, internet, etc., and start thinking for yourself again. Research the coronavirus for yourself and see the truth, and decide for yourself before you allow yourself to be enslaved by your government.

We are afraid of losing because we do not know what we truly possess. We are afraid of thinking for ourselves because we are afraid to fail. We are afraid of standing out in the crowd because we do not know who we indeed are. We are afraid to stand up against wrongdoings because we do not know what we believe in. Now we are dictated by fear; it has become our most excellent drug-filled pacifier that we allow the government to stick in our mouth every time we open it so that we will be good little children and do as we are told.

Welcome to the zombie apocalypse, my American brothers and sisters. Are you willing to partake in this insanity? Or are we going to take a stand and do something about it? Let us start by refusing to be placed into a box that's anything other than Free American.

Epilogue

On June 29, 2020, I had the honor of participating with Vice President Pence in a meeting in the White House. Here a small group of thought leaders considered next steps toward racial conciliation. Just the day before I had completed the text for this book and realized at this meeting that the issue of what we need in leadership from President Trump and Vice President Pence had been left unaddressed. This book requires an Epilogue.

Thomas Jefferson wrote: "The ground of liberty is to be gained by inches." The first step toward liberty was to rise from a coastal string of British colonies to become a sovereign nation. The single founding principle of the new republic was liberty, and the Constitution outlined the means through which liberty could yet be further expanded.

Years later the sixteenth occupant of the White House wrote: "Those who deny freedom to others, deserve it not for themselves; and, under a just God can not long retain it." Through the convulsion of the Civil War, at last African Americans were held as free and equal citizens under the law and the great mantle of chattel slavery was removed.

Now, what about our time? What do these epochal times demand as the struggle for the ground of liberty continues? As was the case for Presidents Jefferson and Lincoln, words matter. We are entering a time when the very continuance of the nation is threatened. A generation principally understands President Jefferson as a slaveholder, and the statue of President Lincoln needs protection from being toppled by enraged protestors. Does President Trump have a hold on history sufficient to navigate these roiled waters?

The first ingredient of greatness is humility. As we advance ourselves, we become less effective in advancing our cause. The president has been a very effective advocate for African Americans. His policies of tax cuts, regulation reduction, and judicial reform have resulted in plummeting unemployment among black Americans, enhanced prosperity, and support of the faith-based institutions that are pillars of the African American community. This is an enviable record and arguably a godsend compared to the impact his predecessor had on black America.

How these achievements are presented, though, makes all the difference. His support for historically black colleges can be related through stories of young people of limited financial means now newly able to fulfill their professional dreams; criminal reform allowing for reunited families; enterprise zones spurring black women to start new businesses. Let the victories of these citizens establish the rightness of these policies. Humility invites people into the room; hubris empties it out. In Jeremiah we are instructed to not let "the wise man boast in his wisdom, let not the mighty man boast in his might, let not the rich man boast in his riches." We ignore these precepts at our own peril. As soon as the story becomes about us, it is no longer of interest.

The second ingredient of greatness is steadfastness. People about whom we think highly are in general people with core values evident throughout their lives. In gazing up at the Pole Star, John Keats wrote: "Bright star, would I were stedfast as thou art . . ." In the same way that the boat with the deep keel stays steady on its course, likewise the leader guided by firm convictions is unswerving in his direction.

President Jefferson advanced liberty; President Lincoln preserved the nation; President Reagan opposed communism. Having these ideas as the ground basis of their identities allowed these leaders to stay on task despite the vicissitudes of the moment that might draw lesser men to sway. The president needs now to share with us those core values which likely most Americans will share with him. The vision for the next four years needs to be predicated on the foundation of these animating principles. Rarely in a political campaign is it enough to persuade voters to vote against your opponent. Winners provide the voters with reason to support them.

The final ingredient of greatness is honesty. Mark Twain once wrote: "When in doubt tell the truth. It will confound your enemies and astound your friends." While an honest politician is nearly an oxymoron, still the practical value of straightforward truth-telling is immense. Perhaps President Nixon might have completed his second term with an admission to the Watergate bugging and a proper sense of contrition. President Reagan conceded to the mistake of Iran Contra and owned the error, ending the travail. What national agony could potentially have been avoided had President Clinton admitted to his sexual indiscretion amidst his popular tenure?

Perhaps our moment is the ripest for the transformative power of honesty. The country is caught in a swirl of uncertainty. People of all races are now engaged in a fevered conversation about police brutality, embedded prejudice, and unequal justice. Many are new to the conversation and are honestly making forays into these territories for the first time and with unformed opinions. They are willing to be led. However, people will not be led unless they first trust. The president now speaking candidly, reflectively, and modestly, inviting others to the table and letting the conversation lead where it may, is the bromide of our time. Maya Angelou wrote that "the caged bird sings of freedom." This is the song that now needs to be heard.

My father, James Stirk Williams, and mother, Thelma Howard Williams.

Acknowledgments

Dedicated to my beloved deceased parents, James Stirk and Thelma Howard Williams. Always my best role and goal models.

Thank you, Justice Clarence Thomas, Dr. Benjamin Carson, David Smith, C. Boyden Gray, Terry Giles, and Adean Wells King. Always my lifelong and trusted brothers for their unconditional support system.

Mary and Logan Taylor, my sister and my niece, the apples of my eyes.

Bryan Donohue for being my moral compass during the writing of this book.

Travis Stephens for challenging me to think outside of the box.

Robert J. Brown for his years of friendship and guidance.

My secret strength through all the years, Shirley E. Dave.

Shermichael Singleton for the enormous dedication and for motivating me to complete this book in two weeks.

I also want to thank the publisher Skyhorse, and especially editor Hector Carosso.

To my company, Howard Stirk Holdings, that bears the name of my parents.